D1484629

GABRIEL DUMONT SPEAKS

"Gabriel Dumont, French half breed, Riel's Second in Command 1885 Rebellion."
Glenbow Archives, Calgary (NA 1177-1).

GABRIEL DUMONT SPEAKS

Revised second edition

Translated by Michael Barnholden

 Talonbooks

Talonbooks
Box 2076, Vancouver, British Columbia, Canada V6B 3S3
www.talonbooks.com

Typeset in Minion and Meta. Printed and bound in Canada.

First printing, second edition: 2009

The publisher gratefully acknowledges the financial support of the Canada Council for the Arts; the Government of Canada through the Book Publishing Industry Development Program; and the Province of British Columbia through the British Columbia Arts Council and the Book Publishing Tax Credit for our publishing activities.

Library and Archives Canada Cataloguing in Publication

Dumont, Gabriel, 1837–1906
  Gabriel Dumont speaks / Gabriel Dumont ; translated by Michael Barnholden. — Rev. ed.

Translated from the French.
ISBN 978-0-88922-625-8

1. Dumont, Gabriel, 1837–1906. 2. Riel Rebellion, 1885—Personal narratives. 3. Métis—Canada, Western—Biography. I. Barnholden, Michael, 1951– II. Title.

FC3217.1.D84A3 2009   971.05'4092   C2009-902890-5

for Nancy, all ways,
and the Kootenay School of Writing, of course

Table of Contents

Acknowledgements

Karl Siegler, publisher of Talonbooks, and I have had a near forty-year conversation about Gabriel Dumont, and the Métis. Without his exceptional editorial skills and continuing engagement, this book would not be what it is. I value his friendship beyond words.

Introduction

Text and Context

Gabriel Dumont Speaks is an English-language interpretation of two closely related documents: "Le récit de Gabriel Dumont" and "Les mémoires dictés par Gabriel Dumont" completed in 1903, and held in the archives of the Société historique de Saint-Boniface. I use the term "interpretation" because what I have attempted to create in this book is not a literal translation of these documents, but a re-creation of a key moment in the oral history of Canada. I chose *Gabriel Dumont Speaks* for the title to foreground and to demonstrate the fact that, historically, Gabriel Dumont was much more than the voiceless, one-dimensional adjutant general of the 1885 "Métis Rebellion" led by Louis Riel, as he is so often portrayed in our history books: he was, first and foremost, a political and cultural leader of the Métis people, and his historic dictations reveal him to be a man of considerable intellectual power, as well as a redoubtable man of action.

Words on paper, books, are the intellectual currency of Western culture. The chief intent of this book is therefore to re-create the voice of Gabriel Dumont—to make him an author—and to give his words the legitimacy that authorship entails in our culture. The photographic images I have chosen to include with Dumont's recitations capture perfectly this complexity of his character—he is equally at home on the Prairies, in the high-society parlours of Eastern Canada, and in Buffalo Bill's Wild West Show—he has both the capacity and the ability to constantly and effectively adapt to his environment. The widely held notion that Dumont represents the passing of an era—the wilderness man who cannot adapt to the encroachments of civilization—could not be further from the historical truth. If anything, Dumont represents an image of the archetypal hero buried deep within Western culture, and like all such heroes, he embodies the apotheosis of an ideal, an ideal he is willing to fight for. He is loyal to a fault, following Riel's strategies even when he knows they mean certain loss for his people.

For the Métis, Dumont is a hero with little or no ambiguity about his character, but much can and has been read into his received personality outside the frame of his own culture. He is a hero to many: battling through serious injury against overwhelming odds in the War of 1885; a romantic figure whose loving wife dies an early death after joining him in exile; leading an under-equipped, poorly armed, vastly outnumbered army against the state and winning all except the last battle; his public image defines a certain uncanny determination in the face of overwhelming odds. Chairman Mao and Ho Chi Minh are said to have studied his guerrilla tactics. To anarchists he is an archetypal indigenous resistance fighter.

But all of these stereotypes, however flattering and noble, have served primarily to erase Gabriel Dumont's own experiences and words from our history books. If we want to know what he thought about the important issues and events in which he was involved, he will tell us— it's all there in his memoirs—and in coming to know it, we must recognize the fact that his voice is not as conclusive as we might have wished it to be. Though one can extract from that voice support for many of our received images of him, he does not always say what we might want to hear from him, if we let him speak—he is as deeply human and full of contradictions as we, his listeners from all cultures, continue to be. Even the narrative is not always reliable. When Dumont states that he did not go to Europe with Buffalo Bill because he had not been granted amnesty, the dates are contradictory: Buffalo Bill's Wild West Show visited England in 1887 and toured Europe in 1889. Dumont was granted amnesty in 1886. While this discrepancy might have resulted from a simple transcription error, the reference is unclear and is impossible to decipher.

His public persona remains, however, almost always tied to Louis Riel. In 1869–70 he offers, probably through intermediaries, to "bring the Indians" when Riel and his government are threatened in what was to become Manitoba. It is Dumont who rides to Montana to convince

Mrs. Riboulet and Gabriel Dumont, Staten Island, New York, 1887.
Library and Archives Canada, Ottawa (A8211).

Métis Council minutes, St. Antony, March 21, 1885.
Library and Archives Canada, Ottawa.

Riel to return to the Northwest Territories to help negotiate with the Canadian government. Riel and Dumont, the political and the war chiefs respectively, lead the Métis Nation at Batoche against the North West Field Force of Canada when "justice commands us to take up arms." Dumont sees Louis Riel for the final time in 1885 just before Riel surrenders to the Canadian military, but unlike Riel, Dumont escapes across the medicine line to the United States. Rumours persist that Dumont organized a jailbreak to spring Riel from custody and spirit him out of the country after he is sentenced to hang. In 1887 and 1888, Dumont tours Québec, eloquently speaking to the issues raised by Riel's hanging for treason, a hot issue in Québec politics, and it is here that he dictated to a group of journalists and politicians the first of what would eventually become two memoirs of the "Riel Rebellion." On this occasion, his story was written down by B.A.T. Montigny, of Québec City. The dictation was read back to him for his approval and, after being edited by Adolphe Ouimet, was privately published as part of *La vérité sur la question métisse au Nord-Ouest* (1889). The book, long out of print, is a polemic that was used in an attempt to advance the fortunes of the Québec Liberal Party using Riel's name as a rallying cry. Sixty years later, G.E.G. Stanley translated this first Dumont memoir into English and it was published in the 1949 issue of the *Canadian Historical Review*—an obscure publication perhaps, but not so arcane as to be unavailable in the libraries of any large Canadian city. It has since been extensively quoted in almost every Anglophone work on Riel, and on many other aspects of the "Métis Rebellion."

However, sometime in 1902 or 1903—the exact date is uncertain—a representative of L'Union nationale métisse de Saint-Joseph transcribed the second of Gabriel Dumont's two memoirs, which, until very recently, remained almost completely unknown to historians. The original manuscripts of Dumont's dictations "Récit" and "Dictés," dated 1903, were kept in the archive of L'Union nationale métisse de Saint-Joseph, until they were transferred to the Provincial Archives of Manitoba. They have now been returned to L'Union nationale métisse de Saint-Joseph and reside in the archives of the Société historique de Saint-Boniface. The manuscripts consist of 103 handwritten pages, of the same size for the most part, although at least two pages have been torn from other, smaller sources. A quill pen was used, and the handwriting appears to be that of one person, whose identity is not known. The dictation may have taken place on more than one occasion, perhaps on two consecutive evenings: there are two "page ones," but neither is the first page. The first twelve pages serve as an introduction, and reflect the evening's preliminaries: a small group has gathered, opening remarks are made, questions are asked and answered, and the tone of the narrative is set. The handwriting is cramped, suggesting that the writer is rushing to keep up with Dumont's speech. The most awkward part of the transcription is the way the recorder chooses to handle the narrative. Dumont must have spoken in the first-person, but the narrative is written in the third-person. It is my guess that French, the transcriber's first language, was Dumont's second or third. The text refers to Dumont's ability to speak Cree and Sioux, and implies he knew Blackfoot. He may have delivered this dictation in what linguists refer to as "incipient Michif," the syntax of which is certainly not typically French, but more akin to Cree, although there are no Cree words in what was recorded. Perhaps the transcriber also spoke Michif and rendered it into his tortuous French as he wrote. It seems most likely that some language differences between Dumont and the person recording his speech made the task of transcription exceedingly difficult.

Since these two pieces of manuscript along with some accompanying miscellaneous notes titled "general information" are intimately related in every way and can function as one discrete work, I set out to gather them under one title and ascribe their authorship to Gabriel Dumont. It was my intention to return the recorded words spoken on that occasion to Dumont: to make him, who had never had the opportunity to learn to read nor write, the author of his own story—to redress his image as that of entirely a man of action—and restore to him his intellectual and political standing. Of course, I wanted the work to be available in my own first language—English—not only because it is an interesting story, but more importantly to clarify Dumont's status within the Métis nation for a wider Canadian community. It is not necessary to speculate in regards to Dumont's life, experiences and accomplishments when we can simply read his words.

Until 1993 this second of Gabriel Dumont's accounts of his life was not widely known at all. I happened on it by mistake when in 1971 I requested the "Dumont memoir" from the national archives, thinking I was asking for the transcript of his first dictation in 1887–88. What arrived in the mail instead was a photostat of 103 handwritten pages from a variety of notebooks and scraps of paper. The writing varied from easily legible to almost impossible to read. I began immediately to translate these mysterious manuscripts and soon realized they were not written in standard French, not even seventy-year-old standard French. I initially assumed that the dictation had been done in Michif, the everyday language of the South Branch Métis with its French nouns and Cree verbs and sentence structure. What was written was not, however, Michif but rather what I now know to be Michif-French. I also realized right away that this was not the original of the dictation I had been looking for. I had wanted to compare the original first dictation of 1887–88 (at the time the only one I knew existed) to both the widely disseminated 1889 publication, *La verité sur la question métisse au Nord-Ouest*, and to its English translation published in 1949.

In short, I was not sure what I had received, so I began to look for the source of the manuscript I had in hand. This was far more difficult before the days of the Internet, and I had few resources to help me in this search. About half way through I gave up. I also knew by then that I would not use this account as the basis of a novel or a narrative poem, as had been my naïve intent at the time—there was no way I could ever match the power of Dumont's original narrative.

Twenty years later I came back to the project, having decided that even a journeyman translation of this mysterious document was better than no translation at all. The story it contained was not only important but it was well told, and I thought perhaps the publication of an English version of the manuscripts might act as a catalyst to flush out the details that continued to elude me, from other individuals who had perhaps also grappled with this text. One of the interesting things about history is that (despite recent neo-liberal claims to the contrary) it is never over: history is constantly being rewritten as new material is found and new interpretations of older materials open up. Out of this process, during which I made the key decision to restore the narrative of the manuscript from the third-person to the first-, came the first edition of *Gabriel Dumont Speaks*, published by Talonbooks in 1993.

In 2006, Les Éditions du Blé of Saint Boniface, Manitoba, published a bilingual edition of this work titled *Gabriel Dumont: Mémoires*, edited and annotated by Denis Combet, and translated by Lise Gaboury-Diallo. This handsome, well-illustrated volume provides an authoritative French language script of the two dictations—*Memoirs as Dictated by Gabriel Dumont* and *Gabriel Dumont's Story*—as well as an English translation of them.

Working from the original transcriptions, the editor and translator of *Gabriel Dumont: Mémoires* have established a worthy scholarly reference text. Faced with similar choices that I had to make when I originally began work on my "interpretation," they have decided to name Dumont as the author, yet left the text in the third-person, crediting an anonymous author/transcriber with its creation. This is, of course, a valid scholarly necessity but leaves open enough ambiguity for what I have proposed, which is to both attribute its authorship to Dumont and to return the text to his first-person voice. I consider it a strong possibility that Dumont would have wanted it that way, and it remains unclear why the transcriber chose to render Dumont's speech in the third-person. The work of Professors Combet and Gaboury-Diallo on the original manuscript has also allowed me to make corrections to the portions of the transcript I received from the National Archives of Canada in 1971 that had remained unreadable to me, and clarified the order of the pages that was apparently incorrect when I originally received them.

With the publication of *Gabriel Dumont: Mémoires* in 2006, I finally felt free from slavishly adhering to the order of the text as originally presented to me in 1971: consequently I have made several changes to my first (1993) edition of *Gabriel Dumont Speaks* that benefit the narrative considerably. The presence of the definitive new scholarly text also allows me more freedom to interpret some of the elements of the original transcript, and I have excercised that freedom, I hope, to good effect.

The order in which I received the manuscript did make some sense if one understood it as having been dictated on two separate occasions, the first being an introductory session in which the transcriber was getting up to speed on Dumont's life and some of the events after Riel's surrender. It seems to me, however, the question of whether or not these stories were dictated to whom is clearly the same person at slightly different times is of little importance. That the two pieces of manuscript are distinct does not mean they should be separated: in fact they inform one another, and the new order proposed by the scholarly edition doesn't really detract from the order I proposed in my first edition, and to a certain degree maintain in this second edition of *Gabriel Dumont Speaks*. Initially by chance, and now by choice, there are in fact three sections to the narrative as I have interpreted it: an introductory biographical section; then the rebellion narrative up to and including Dumont's separation from Riel; followed by miscellaneous stories, bits and pieces that in fact should more properly be seen as appendices to the main, chronological narrative. Then we have an order that works for me: Dumont's early life, the War of 1885, and an appendix of contextualizing afterthoughts.

Gabriel Dumont

Gabriel Dumont was born in what is now Winnipeg in 1837 or 1838, fourth of the eleven children (five girls and six boys) of Isidore Dumont and Louise Laframboise. Like his father had been before him, Isidore became the head of the Dumont band. His father, Jean-Baptiste Dumont, had come west from Québec in the 1790s and married Josette Sarcisse, a Sarcee woman. When Gabriel was two, his father decided to leave the farm where he had three acres under cultivation, and become an independent trader in the Fort Pitt area. From then on, Gabriel's childhood was spent moving back and forth across the prairie following the hunt and learning the skills associated with that life.

In 1858 Gabriel Dumont met and married Madeleine Wilkie, daughter of buffalo hunter and trader Jean-Baptiste Wilkie and his Indian wife Isabella Azure, and continued to fashion a life based on his hunting prowess. Because the hunt took him from the Red River to the foot of the Rockies and back, he always did a little trading on the side with

NOTICE.

Gabriel's Crossing.

The public are informed that GABRIFL'S Crossing is now in readiness for the accommodation of the public.

One Scow, the Best on the River,

will be in constant readiness. The road by this ferry is the SHORTEST by twenty-five miles going to or going east from Battleford.

The public promptly attended to.

GABRIEL DUMONT.

May, 1880.   45

Sign for Gabriel's Ferry on the South Saskatchewan River.

Glenbow Archives, Calgary (NA-1829-5).

the Blackfoot, Sioux and Crow, and he appears to have become conversant in all their languages. At the time he, in turn, was elected chief of the band in 1863, the Dumonts were using the Batoche area as a winter camp, and by 1868 the decision was made to move and settle there permanently. As head of the Dumont band, Gabriel presided over the hunt, negotiated peace treaties and formed alliances with other prairie nations. As more and more settlers took up homesteads in the South Saskatchewan River area, commercial activity grew, the territorial government became increasingly active, and Dumont's leadership took on a political and diplomatic role, culminating in his election as president of the short-lived St. Laurent Council in December of 1873. Diplomacy does not seem to have been Dumont's favourite part of the job—his patience, especially with government bureaucracy, was short at best. Following the hunt, trading a little, hauling some freight and even guiding missionaries took care of his material needs quite well. Dumont eventually got title to the property where the south branch of the Carlton Trail crossed the South Saskatchewan River. With experience as a hunter and warrior of the Great Plains, he now also became a politician and a small businessman, running a trading post beside his home, and a reaction ferry—a scow propelled by the current—across the South Saskatchewan River. His imposing presence named the place, which became known as "Gabriel's Crossing." His wife had a washing machine, while Dumont had a billiard table imported from France.

It has been said that Madeleine Dumont, who unlike Gabriel had had access to schooling, could read, write and speak English, and that she taught school at Batoche in the years before the "rebellion." By the summer of 1884, when the Métis of the Northwest Territories asked Louis Riel to return from exile in the United States to negotiate their grievances, the slate billiard table, which took up most of the store, and the hand-cranked washing machine that eased the domestic burden of their household, were a measure the Dumonts' modest wealth.

In this 1903 dictation, Gabriel Dumont confirms his now legendary offer to "bring the Indians" to reinforce Riel's army at Red River in the "First Riel Rebellion" of 1869–70. Although this present text seems to indicate that Riel did not know Dumont very well, if at all, before 1884, (this seems unlikely, given Dumont's own political status as president of the St. Laurent Council in 1873), it remains a possibility that the offer was made through intermediaries. Certainly during the 1885 "rebellion," Riel knew and trusted Dumont well enough to appoint him adjutant general in charge of the army of the new Métis nation of the Northwest. While the two men differed over tactics and religion, Dumont had always loyally supported the basic ideal Riel espoused—the status of the Métis people as a free and independent nation—and fought long and hard for it. Close to fifty Métis men died during the 1885 war, others were arrested, and many more fled either north to wilder country, or south to the United States, as Dumont did. His wife Madeleine died of tuberculosis shortly after joining him in exile in Montana.

Riel was hanged in November 1885, and the following spring Dumont joined Buffalo Bill's Wild West Show, where he was billed as "The Hero of the Half-breed Rebellion." He stayed with the show until shortly after his pardon in the summer of 1886, after which he took on speaking engagements before French-speaking audiences in the northeastern United States. From late 1887 to early 1888, he helped with Honoré Mercier's election campaign in Québec, which featured as one of its central issues growing public objection to Louis Riel's hanging for treason by Canada. However, Dumont soon began to consider "official" politics and "polite" public speaking as ineffective in the cause of creating and legitimizing a Métis nation. He may have returned to the Wild West Show for a brief period, performing as a marksman and outrider, before heading back west to a cabin on his nephew Alexis Dumont's property near Batoche to resume a life of hunting, fishing and trapping. A photo taken close to this time, in approximately 1900, shows him as a large man in his sixties, wearing a rough suit and vest. His watch chain is draped from a button down to his vest pocket, and two medals are displayed prominently on his chest. He wears a fine black Stetson and carries an ornately carved cane. The once full beard is now trimmed and his chin is bare, but he still wears his riding boots. He has survived and adapted. In six years he will die of natural causes, undefeated.

Unlike Dumont's earlier 1887–88 Québec narrative, which had been solicited, and which was always intended for purely political purposes, what emerges most clearly from Dumont's very personal 1902–03 narrative is his warrior ethos: he is at all times and in all situations ready, willing and able to assert his reputation for fearlessness and bravery. He does not hesitate to contract his services to the territorial government—the same government for which he has organized a replacement provisional government. Early in his life he serves as a lieutenant in the local militia. His family is closely allied with both the Cree and the Sioux, and he fights with the Cree against the Blackfoot for no other reason than to earn from them a degree of respect that supercedes their own law. The petitions he organizes always place the needs of the Indians first. Many do not understand his willingness to be "exploited" and "humiliated" by Buffalo Bill's Wild West Show, which featured him as "The Hero of the Half-breed Rebellion," but these are retrospective twenty-first century value-judgments that Gabriel Dumont simply does not know or would not share, as his story "Episodes of my Life" makes clear. To him, the Show merely offers an opportunity to earn income, while displaying his prowess as a horseman and marksman—a prowess he takes for granted, as does he his proud mixed-blood heritage. He is Métis both in culture and in race, and he marries within the mixed-race community. The history of his family in the west is a map of proud anti-colonialism. His people have learned both the old and the new ways of the "new land"—both in terms of its languages and its cultures. They participate fully in the new piece-work economy, supplying the Hudson's Bay Company (HBC) with meat and furs, while despising the employer that exploits them—they have learned to live with that. But when the Canadian Pacific Railway (CPR) and its attendant "civilizing institutions" of land surveys and regulation of natural resources, such as land, water and trees, arrives on the Prairies, and begins to change the very foundations of the local political economy, particularly with respect to the rights of land tenure, this is simply asking too much. However, between 1867 and 1885 the Métis were increasingly being asked to bear these encroachments. The circumstances forcing them to take up their own, previously shared land, re-surveyed as private property, to farm it, pay for wood cut on crown land, and give up the hunt, lead to the destruction of their hybrid way of life.

Gabriel Dumont with Buffalo Bill's Wild West Show.
Glenbow Archives, Calgary (NA-4635-1).

Gabriel Dumont around 1900.
Library and Archives Canada, Ottawa (C-5817).

Louis Riel

Louis Riel was never a hunter, but rather a son of the Red River Settlement. His father, Louis Riel Sr., had married into one of the original settler families, the Lagimodières, in 1812. Louis Riel Sr. was a miller and political organizer known particularly for his support of Guillaume Sayer's challenge to the HBC's fur-trade monopoly. His son Louis was born on October 22, 1844. Following his early schooling with the Catholic priests at Saint Boniface, Bishop Tache arranged for Riel to attend the Sulpician Order's Petit Séminaire of the Collège de Montréal in Québec. After his father's death in 1864, he withdrew and began attending the Grey Nuns School where he was expelled for disciplinary reasons. He began working as a law clerk in the Montréal offices of Rodolphe Laflamme. Soon disappointed in love and tired of legal work, he left Montréal in early 1868, eventually returning to the Red River Settlement on July 26, 1868.

The transfer of Rupert's Land from the Hudson's Bay Company to Canada in 1868 and the concomitant influx of Anglophone Canadian settlers increased tension in the Red River Settlement. The match that sparked the "First Riel Rebellion" was the arrival, by order of the Canadian Minister of Public Works, of a survey party. The Métis majority, which had not been consulted about the survey, was upset by the impending project: not only did the survey mean the Métis did not have "legal" title to their lands, but it intended to divide property into sections in the American grid style, thereby over-riding the existing Métis system in which every lot had river access. Riel denounced the survey and helped disrupt the surveyors' work, becoming secretary of the "Métis National Committee," whose position was that Canada must negotiate with the Métis before assuming authority in the settlement. When the Canadian governor designate attempted to enter the territory, he and his party were turned back at the border and the Métis seized Fort Garry. Riel invited all residents of the Red River Settlement to a convention where he presented a list of rights that would serve as conditions for the settlement's union with Canada. A small number of settlers loyal to Britain and Ottawa, known as the "Canadian Party," resisted this initiative, and were arrested and held in Upper Fort Garry by the Métis National Committee, which on December 8 declared a provisional government. Louis Riel became its president on December 27. Negotiations with a delegation from Ottawa began in early January, and by early February a list of rights had been agreed upon and representatives had been elected to proceed to Ottawa for direct negotiations with Canada. Shortly before the delegation left the settlement, Riel had allowed the execution of an Orangeman, Thomas Scott, one of the prisoners, for defying the authority of the provisional government. This presented serious difficulties for the negotiators, but by May, the Manitoba Act formally admitting Manitoba into Canada was passed by Parliament. Unfortunately no amnesty for members of the provisional government was included in the act. The Canadian government sent a military expedition to the Red River Settlement, and rumours of plans by the militia to lynch Riel prompted him to go into exile in the Dakota Territory across the international border.

He returned to Manitoba frequently, even winning a seat in federal Parliament three times, although he was never able to take his seat. He lived in fear of arrest and/or assassination (at one point, Ontario had placed a bounty on his head) until eventually Parliament granted him amnesty in 1875, provided he remained in exile for five more years. Those five years were marked by his hospitalization for mental instability and wandering.

Ending up in Montana as a trader and interpreter, he married Marguerite Monet (dit Bellehumeur) in 1881. They had three children, two boys and a girl; Riel became an American citizen; and he began to teach school and write out his ideas for a new Métis society in the Northwest at St. Peter's Mission, where Dumont and his party found him in 1884.

Dumont and Riel represent two different Métis experiences in the west. Riel managed to negotiate Métis entry into Canada in the Red River in 1870, and founded a new religion, albeit with only one baptized adherent. Dumont chose a different "negotiation with civilization" by ranging further west to the valley of the South Saskatchewan River. The two men's lives are intertwined not just because they are Métis, but rather because they operated publically in one overlapping endeavour: politics. Privately, they each lived completely different lives: for Riel, spirituality and the Church was his main interest, whereas Dumont lived in the natural world of the hunt, of which war is a subset. Their worlds overlapped in the Saskatchewan Territory of Canada in 1885, where both men would make their last stand at Batoche in an ongoing defence of the Métis Nation.

Métissage

Becoming Métis, or "métissage" as it is sometimes called, is a process of blending cultures. In some of its particulars the process of métissage may look like colonization, but in fact it is very different. If the Métis had been regarded as a nation similar to the other First Nations on the prairie, as separate and distinct as the Cree or the Sioux to whom they were closely related, post-contact history in Canada would have been seen in a very different light. The Métis were in fact an entirely unique people in the history of the colonization of the Americas, whose culture, values and politics were a synthesis of those of the native Plains people, and the white, usually Francophone settlers who arrived on the Prairies after the first wave of explorers. This wave of settlers was for the most part made up of fur trade workers, often little more than indentured servants to the Hudson's Bay Company or the North West Company, some of whom chose to remain on the prairie. Intermarriage with these new immigrants became a common practice among most of the Great Plains tribes, particularly the Cree. When white fur-traders first came to the west in the 1700s, those who wished to stay were welcomed, and this welcome was extended to the settlers that followed, creating a third nation on the Prairies—a distinct culture that was an adaptive, cooperative hybrid between the advancing white and the retreating Indian cultures. The Métis soon became leaders among all the prairie First Nations, in their resistance to the cultural and corporate invasion led by the Church, the fur trade companies and the CPR, sponsored and supported by the expansionist ambitions of the new Dominion of Canada since 1867.

The Métis created a unique language and culture by borrowing elements from other languages and cultures, and adapting them to suit their socio-economic circumstances, chief among these being: the annual buffalo hunt; trade with and for the North West Company and the Hudson's Bay Company; and some farming, using the Québec habitant model of narrow lots with water access, along the Red, Assiniboine and Saskatchewan Rivers—the main communication and transportation routes for the Métis. While the Métis of the Batoche area probably spoke a form of incipient Michif, a dialect combining Cree sentence structure and verb forms with French nouns, Cree was the first language of the Dumont band. Most of those tried after the war who could be considered members of the Dumont band elected to be tried in Cree. Thus, while it can be said that Métis culture was syncretic in essence, there is no question that its predominant elements were native. The social organization of Métis society can therefore best be compared to that of its neighbouring and related First Nations, rather than to that of colonial cultures in French and English Canada.

By the mid-1800s, at the latest, there were at least two distinct Métis cultures: the settled Métis and the "wild" or free Métis of the Plains, who chose to leave the Red River and move further west and north rather than settle in one place. By 1884 the Métis were far from homogeneous. There were those who lived in two-storey houses, working as freighters and traders, those who lived in tipis and subsisted on the hunt, and still others who had become treaty Indians. Some worked for the government as agricultural instructors (although very few Métis were farmers) or as clerks and interpreters. Métis life was originally based on sharing vast areas of public land as needed. But the buffalo hunt gradually ended—the last one left Batoche in 1882 and returned with only eleven animals. As the land base began to shrink, and the buffalo disappeared, Métis culture faced the inevitability of change. Eventually a broad-based political consensus developed, having as its main concern land tenure for all residents of the Northwest—Métis, Indians and other settlers, including the English of the Prince Albert district. Under the leadership of Dumont and others, petitions were presented to both the appointed territorial and federal governments in Ottawa; however no replies were ever received. It is clear that the Métis were willing to negotiate by treaty, nation to nation: Riel wrote to Sir

John A. Macdonald at one point informing him of Dumont's anger over the government's offer of a treaty to every minor chief but him.

Riel was an educated, settled Métis who had negotiated a treaty, nation to nation, with the new country of Canada in 1869–70, an accomplishment that caused him to be seen as the "Social or Political Chief" of the Métis. Dumont, on the other hand, was seen as a "wild" Métis, chief of his band, and for his well-known feats of bravery was accorded the status of "War Chief." This delegation of roles parallels the relative positions taken by the Cree's Big Bear and Wandering Spirit.

Having learned from his previous experience in Manitoba in 1869–70, Louis Riel considered threatening force in order to further negotiations with Canada, but he underestimated the level of frustration among the territorial Métis in 1884–85. Finally, according to Dumont, it was Riel himself who first raised the possibility of another "rebellion" in 1885. From that point on, Gabriel Dumont the war chief took over and horses, rifles, even sticks and stones, became the weapons of the Métis in their battle with the government of Canada—only after all negotiations, including those with Riel, had ended unsuccessfully. The individual citizen was free to follow either chief, as far as he or she wished.

It is clear from Dumont's second account, however, that the Métis fought in the manner of the Indians. Although he had some militia training, Dumont saw war through Indian eyes—not from the perspective of the then very "modern" Major General Frederick Middleton, veteran of many English campaigns and the commander of the Canadian forces during the "1885 Rebellion." Short, quick engagements, often executed at night by a highly mobile force that knew the country well—essentially guerrilla tactics—was probably the only strategy the Métis could have used to hold their ground for a time against the untried, hastily gathered Canadian troops. What surprised the Métis was the large number of white men, well-equipped with guns, food and transportation, who were put in the field, and the length of time they were prepared to simply sit and wait.

Conclusion

Gabriel Dumont recited his own history—and Métis history—with great dignity. He was an old warrior telling tales of bravery and daring, speaking from his heart, unconcerned with conforming to established "truth." Both his story, and having the opportunity to tell it, mattered to him. I believe that he would have wanted this piece widely disseminated. This document, which I believe to be in the public domain, languished for ninety years in the archives, and is now available in the original and in two English versions: the word-for-word literal translation and my variant interpretation.

The most compelling difference between Dumont's oral history and the accepted version of the Métis story lies in Dumont's views on the "rebellion." He saw it not as a French revolt against English Canadian authority, but rather as a war between two nations: an indigenous people, with broad local support, fighting to repel an uncompromising, overwhelming invader who disregarded the concerns of the people it had assumed the authority to govern in fulfilment of its self-declared manifest destiny of creating a "Dominion from Sea to Sea."

This document preserves an unrepeatable oral occasion, and offers us the rare opportunity to view one of the central events in the history of the Métis as perceived by one of their key heroes. The War of 1885 has of course been much documented by the dominant culture, but its historians rely primarily on written sources, and largely ignore the contributions of oral historians like Gabriel Dumont. Unfortunately, "oral culture" is too often equated with "illiterate," and therefore "backward," culture. Together with "oral history," terms like "primitive" and "aboriginal" are frequently used in a derogatory fashion, while "literate," "developed" and "civilized" are privileged by a dominant culture that somehow deems itself superior by virtue of its print-dependency. When a dominant culture demands cultural conformity, it simultaneously sets out to erase cultural difference. In this context, Gabriel Dumont's grievance, conveyed to John A. Macdonald by the literate Louis Riel, that the Canadian government had made a treaty with every chief on the prairie except him, is much more than the expression of a personal slight.

Historically, the second dictation is interesting on a number of counts, not the least of which is its remaining untranslated and unpublished until 1993. It is referred to in some of the material on Dumont, Riel and the War of 1885, but not always, and certainly not consistently. Sometimes, quotations from this dictation have been excerpted but their source has remained unacknowledged, or they have become secondary references that are not properly attributed. In addition, this second dictation seems to have been confused with the first on occasion. Why most historians have chosen not to acknowledge the 1903 document is puzzling, unless we consider how it might have been incompatible with the officially received written version of the history it recounts. Dumont's 1887–88 dictation slotted quite neatly into an electoral political agenda, and thus is useful for historical research that continues to serve similar purposes—in no way does it contradict the official historical record. Dumont's second dictation, however contradicts, or certainly questions, much of what is popularly believed about the Métis and their "rebellion."

The validity and reliability of oral history have long been disputed. Dumont's second dictation contains information not included in the first—a discrepancy that raises the question of oral history's validity in a somewhat different way: Dumont's claim that the Canadian troops used explosive bullets against the Métis is seldom mentioned in any work on the "rebellion." In the tradition of written history, this kind of revision would be considered "true" if a substantial enough paper trail were amassed to successfully alter the "facts." This type of "evidence," however, is absent—by definition—in an oral culture, and consequently the revised histories that emerge in such a tradition are regarded with suspicion by historians: they are considered to be mutable, open to improvised "improvements." But this assumption ignores circumstances that could legitimately account for such "revisions"—the oral historian, for example, can obtain new facts or evidence by others (data is as important to the oral historian's process of gathering information as signed and witnessed documents are to that of print-oriented historians). This second dictation by Gabriel Dumont is a much more politically trenchant text than the first because of the way it unsettles the existing historical record. Although over one hundred years have passed since Dumont gave his second dictation, the issues he raised have yet to be adequately addressed by any Canadian government. When Gabriel Dumont speaks, we listen, and we can hear eerie echoes between his story and history. We continue to ignore his story at our peril.

Métis Timeline

1669

Médard Chouart des Groseilliers and his brother-in-law Pierre-Esprit Radisson, who had lived with the Iroquois for two years (they were unlicensed traders who ventured into the fur-trading regions around Lake Michigan and Lake Superior), are fined and have their furs confiscated by authorities in New France who favour agricultural development over trade and exploration. They learn from the Cree that there is better fur country to the north near the "Frozen Sea." After first seeking French backing, and not succeeding in getting support for their expedition, they lead an English fur-trade expedition into Hudson Bay from the north, bypassing the land route from New France. After this successful expedition, the English found the Hudson's Bay Company in 1670.

1670

The Hudson's Bay Company is incorporated by British royal charter in 1670 as The Governor and Company of Adventurers of England trading into Hudson's Bay, and is given Rupert's Land—all of the land draining into Hudson Bay—making it the largest landowner in the world, and the de-facto government of approximately 1.5 million square miles (equivalent to about one third of the area of present-day Canada).

1690–91

Henry Kelsey a.k.a. "the Boy Kelsey," a Hudson's Bay Company employee, explores what is now northern Manitoba from Hudson Bay to the Saskatchewan River. He is generally credited as "the first European to see the Prairies."

1739

François de La Vérendrye accompanies his brother, Louis-Joseph, as they continue their father's search for the Western Sea, and establish French fur-trade posts throughout the area north and west of Lake Superior, and travel to the Saskatchewan River. From there, they eventually reach the Rocky Mountains.

1776–78

Peter Pond—an American partner in the founding of the North West Company, which began as a loose association of Montréal merchants as early as 1770—winters at a fur-trade post he creates at the junction of the Sturgeon and North Saskatchewan Rivers near present-day Prince Albert, Saskatchewan.

1783

The North West Company, operating since 1770 as a loose affiliation of quasi-independent adventurers and traders, is incorporated, with its head office in Montréal. Unlike most HBC employees, the "Nor' Westers" typically shared in their corporation's profits and ventured out to meet indigenous hunter-traders rather than waiting in forts for annual trade visitations.

1812

Lord Selkirk invests significantly in the Hudson's Bay Company in order to acquire 116,000 square miles of land—the Territory of Assiniboia. He establishes an agricultural colony for displaced Scottish Highlanders near the forks of the Red and Assiniboine Rivers, which becomes known as the Red River Settlement.

1816

The war between the two large rival fur-trading companies—the Hudson's Bay Company and the North West Company—culminates in the Battle of Seven Oaks. The Nor' Westers want, at the very least, freedom to travel in HBC-controlled country. Under Cuthbert Grant, the Métis seized a supply of pemmican that the HBC had stolen from them and are en route to sell it to the North West Company when they are confronted by the HBC: a battle ensues. Robert Semple, a governor of the HBC and governor of the Red River Settlement, is killed along with twenty-two of his men. The Métis are later exonerated of any wrongdoing by a royal commissioner.

1821

Rather than give up its monopoly, the HBC is able to extend its holdings north to the Arctic Ocean and west to the Pacific Ocean by agreeing to merge with the North West Company. They also agree to a profit-sharing plan with some of their employees. The newly expanded and reorganized HBC still encounters competition from both American and "Canadian" independent traders who regularly challenge the HBC monopoly in Rupert's Land. The new HBC trade area covers three million square miles.

1837

Gabriel Dumont is born in what is now Winnipeg.

1844

Louis Riel is born at the Red River Settlement, in what is now Saint Boniface.

1849

Louis Riel Sr. leads Métis in defense of Guillaume Sayer and his challenge to the HBC monopoly on fur trading. Although Sayer is found guilty of illegal trading of furs—he was trading into the United States—under pressure from the Métis, the judge levies no fines or punishment, setting a precedent that the HBC could no longer use the courts to enforce their monopoly. In practice there is now finally free trade in Rupert's Land.

1851

The Battle of Grand Coteau between Métis buffalo hunters and Sioux in South Dakota results in a peace treaty between the two nations, and free passage on the North American prairie for Métis hunters and settlers.

1858

Gabriel Dumont marries Madeleine Wilkie.

1867

The British North America Act establishes the Dominion of Canada, comprising, at the time, the united provinces of Québec, Ontario, Nova Scotia and New Brunswick. (Prince Edward Island joins this "Confederation" on July 1, 1873.)

1869

In the interim between the HBC handover of Rupert's Land and the Northwest Territories, and the proclamation of Canada's lieutenant governor to take possession of the Northwest on December 1, there is no government on the Canadian prairies other than the National Committee of Métis.

1870

In response to having not been consulted about the 1869 sale of Rupert's Land by the HBC to Canada, the Métis and some Red River Colony settlers establish a provisional government in the North West, with Louis Riel as its elected president. As a result of the provisional government's concerns, the Manitoba Act is given royal assent on May 12, 1870. Taking effect on July 15, 1870, the act creates the province of Manitoba, based on a bill of rights drawn up by Riel that guarantees land and language rights to the Métis.

1873

Gabriel Dumont is appointed president of the St. Laurent Commune, the site of Métis settlement on the South Saskatchewan River, in order to provide effective local government. The Commune mainly manages the buffalo hunt for Métis residents from Tourond's Coulee north to St. Louis.

On September 4, information is sworn and warrants are issued for the arrest of Louis Riel and Ambrose Lepine in the murder of Thomas Scott during the provisional government of 1870. The province of Ontario offers a $5,000 bounty for Riel's capture.

On October 13, Riel is elected as a member of Parliament for Provencher (basically early Manitoba) by acclamation. He does not take his seat and is expelled.

1874

On February 13, Riel is re-elected as a member of Parliament in a Provencher by-election.

On March 30, Riel signs the Parliamentary roll in Ottawa.

On April 9, Parliament passes a motion (124 to 68) that states: "Louis Riel, having fled from justice and having failed to obey an Order of this House that he should attend in his place, Thursday, 9th day of April, 1874, be expelled by this House."

On September 3, Riel is re-elected to Parliament, this time *in absentia*. He does not take his seat.

1875

The St. Laurent Commune disbands after white independent buffalo hunters complain to the territorial government that Dumont and other Métis have demanded they obey local hunting rules. The territorial government promises representative government for the Métis and other settlers, implying that the commune is no longer needed.

Riel is expelled from Parliament again on February 12 and is banished from Canada for five years.

1880

On October 21, a new syndicate known as the Canadian Pacific Railway Company (CPR), comprising George Stephen, James J. Hill, Duncan McIntyre, Richard B. Angus and John Stewart Kennedy, with Donald A. Smith and Norman Kittson as unofficial silent partners, signs a contract with the Macdonald government agreeing to build a railway linking British Columbia to the eastern provinces in exchange for $25,000,000 and 25,000,000 acres of land situated along the railway's intended route. Some of this land is already occupied, without official title, and some of it is Indian reserve land. No consultation takes place with the existing occupants.

Photograph of Riel taken after signing the Parliamentary roll in 1874.
Library and Archives Canada, Ottawa (C-52177).

1881

On February 15, legislation confirming the CPR contract receives royal assent, and the Canadian Pacific Railway Company is officially incorporated the next day.

1884

Gabriel Dumont meets Louis Riel for the first time on June 4 when a party of Métis from Batoche go to summon Riel from Montana, where he had settled since his exile in 1875. They sought Riel's assistance in resuming stalled negotiations with the Canadian government over rights, land and representative government in the Northwest.

1885

A provisional government is established on March 19 at Batoche, run by a governing body of local Métis called the Exovedate (meaning "from the flock"), with Riel as spiritual advisor and Dumont as adjutant general. In late winter and early spring, the Métis fight the North West Mounted Police and Canadian troops at the Battles of Duck Lake, Fish Creek and Batoche. Indians fight Canadian troops at Frog Lake, Cut Knife Hill and Frenchman's Butte. Some of the Indians attempt to join the Métis at Batoche but are unable to affect an armed coalition.

Dumont flees for the American border on May 13. Riel surrenders on May 15. Poundmaker surrenders on May 23. Big Bear surrenders on July 1.

Riel is hanged on November 16.

On November 27, six Cree and two Assiniboine warriors are hanged at Fort Battleford: Kah-Paypamahchukwao (Wandering Spirit); Itka (Crooked Leg); Kit-Ahwah-Ke-Ni (Miserable Man); Pahpah-Me-Kee-Sick (Round the Sky); Manchoose (Bad Arrow); A-Pis-Chas-Koos (Little Bear); Waywahnitch (Man Without Blood); and Nahpase (Iron Body).

1886

Dumont joins Buffalo Bill's Wild West Show.

1887–88

Dumont dictates his first memoir.

1902–03

Dumont dictates his second memoir.

1906

Dumont dies of natural causes and is buried at Batoche.

"Gabriel Dumont, the famous half-breed plainsman, who was the leader of Riel's armed forces in the second rebellion. Photograph taken in Dakota after the Rebellion." University of Manitoba Archives and Special Collections (A. 98-15).

Gabriel Dumont Speaks

GABRIEL DUMONT

I am sixty-five now, forty-seven during the rebellion. I am the son of Isidore Dumont. I was born in Winnipeg. We left there when I was very young and went to the Fort Pitt area where we stayed until I was ten. Then I returned to Winnipeg with my parents. I fired my first shot in a battle with the Sioux when I was twelve.

During the 1870 rebellion, I was camped at Batoche. Before leaving Winnipeg I told Riel, "If it comes to war, send for me and I will come with the Indians."

Episodes of My Life

Once I killed a Blackfoot while I was fighting for the Cree. This Blackfoot was more daring than the rest: he came toward us all alone. I rode down on him. I had a good runner and managed to turn him, but he got away—so I chased him just like a buffalo, going from side to side. When I caught up to him I stuck the barrel of my rifle into his back and fired. He fell forward in front of my horse. At full gallop the surprise made my horse rear violently and almost threw me off backwards. The Blackfoot's pony stayed right beside me. I passed my leg over the neck of my horse and jumped to the ground catching the riderless pony's bridle. Then I returned to check the Blackfoot. He was dead, and that caused me some pain because he had never done anything to me.

But you want to know why I killed him?

Gabriel Dumont at Fort Assiniboine, 1885.
Glenbow Archives, Calgary (NA-1063-1).

This is why. Six or seven Métis tents were camped near a Cree camp. We were on good terms with them. One day when I was not there, a Cree came to my tent and took a good horse I had left chained and locked. He wanted my horse to fight the Blackfoot who were in the area, so he demanded the horse from my wife. She said no. So the Cree said, "If you don't open the lock, I will kill the horse."

My wife did as he told her. When I got back and found this out, I was very angry. That same night the Cree were having a war dance. I went into the lodge and sat among the women and didn't say anything. When they finished dancing I jumped up and joined the warriors and began to speak.

"Friends, I have done this and I have done that. I will fight beside you here and now to show my courage. All my enemies fear me, everyone says that I am the best with a horse and rifle. But today you have done something to offend me. When I wasn't even there, you took my horse. It was not brave to scare my wife. As long as we have been married, we have always been together; whatever is done to my wife is done to me. I have told you what has happened. I will not let it pass."

The Cree said that this was not done to offend me, but that it was their law. Friends and allies were obliged to supply their best horses when they went to war.

"I do not follow your law," I said. "If you want me to go to war with you, there will be no one in front of me when we ride against the enemy. If it was any other way you could come and take my horse. But as long as I am always first to go up against the enemy, then nobody should touch my horses when I am not there."

The next day the Cree fought the Blackfoot and I went to battle with them. That is what led me to chase down the Blackfoot and kill him. I had to show the Cree that I was the best and that they should respect me.

o o o

One day I was out scouting for buffalo. I left my horse tied foot to halter and climbed a butte. I was not quite at the top when I noticed something hiding across from me on the other side among some rocks. I slid down face-first and worked my way behind the hill. It was either a man or a wolf stretched out on its side. If I yelled, a man would listen, and a wolf would run. I watched for a while then cried out. It was a man. He did not move but seemed to listen for a long time. I thought he might be asleep, but I had to see for myself. I went back down, took my horse, went around the base of the two hills, and went to the top of the one where the man slept. If I tried to get too close to him, he might have gotten the jump on me. So I got off my horse and left him behind. When I got closer I saw the man asleep, with his rifle on the ground beside him. I had my rifle in hand, ready to fire. If I woke him he would be scared, and he would go for his gun and shoot me. So I moved closer, quietly, like a wolf, almost right up to him, and took his rifle away slowly and quietly. Then I fell back and put the gun on the ground behind me. Now there would be no danger, so I went ahead and woke him up with my whip. I carried a leather-plaited whip. He was a Gros Ventre. Soon he was on his knees in front of me, his face begging for mercy. I started to laugh and he soon saw that I was not going to hurt him. I sat beside him, keeping my rifle on the other side, took out my pipe and lit it. The Indian took it gladly and smoked deeply. Then his whole body began to shake and he could not hold the pipe. He showed me by signs that that was how much I had scared him. Finally we got up and I led him to his rifle. Then we moved to my horse, which was hobbled. I realized I would have to bend over to untie the legs but I was afraid to try, afraid he would shoot me as I bent over. So I signed to the Gros Ventre that he should go and get his own horse at the bottom of the hill. He did. And to the pain of his horse he left at top speed like the devil was after him. I left soon after.

o o o

Another time, when I was young, I saw a Blood man on the prairie. We rode at each other never doubting the other would turn his bridle first. When I got near I saw that he wouldn't turn away. He was armed, but our meeting had been so quick and unexpected, he did not have time to draw an arrow from his quiver. Seeing this, I did not want to hurt him, just unsaddle him. Now our horses went shoulder to shoulder. The Blood could not stop his horse. I was right beside him so I pulled up on my reins and jumped up behind him. I grabbed both his arms so he could not defend himself. I took him back to camp that way, and gave him a pipe. He smoked it without getting off his horse. Then I told him he could go and he left as fast as the horse could carry him.

Much later when I was making peace between our nations I met my old prisoner in one of their camps. It was twenty years later, and even though the Gros Ventre now had white hair among his black locks I recognized him. He was Bull Hide, a grand chief of his nation.

o o o

I was going to make peace in a Sioux camp, and just as I was leaving the tent where I was staying, bending down through the narrow opening that was closed by a hanging skin, a Sioux hit me over the head with his rifle as he pulled the trigger. I was lucky the shot missed but I was left with a bruise. The other Sioux kicked and beat him with sticks. He had dishonoured them and was driven from camp.

o o o

In 1891 when I was in the United States, I was almost assassinated. I was camped near some other Métis, alone in my tent. During the night I was awakened by a knife blow behind my left ear. I jumped up, throwing off my attacker. I had done him no harm, so why did he want to hurt me? I asked what he was trying to do. "What do you want?" I asked a few times. I wasn't even angry—just surprised to have a man I had never seen before trying to kill me. He was Herculean, armed like a butcher ready to carve.

The assassin stabbed me many times in the back. Finally I managed to pin him with my knees on his shoulders. I grabbed his hands. During the struggle the killer had slashed my stomach twice, once on the left side just below the ribs, and once a bit lower, under the navel. Each wound was about four or five inches long and left big scars. The wounds had a horribly enticing beauty and made a great show on my stomach. I held my assassin in great respect. My right hand was halfway around his throat, and he was gagging. I grabbed the knife with my left hand, cutting the fingers to the bone.

The nearby tents woke to the noise. When they saw me almost choking my enemy they pulled me off him and let him go. He fled.

I think it was somebody after the $5,000.00 prize the government had put on my head.

My Wound at the Battle of Duck Lake

I suffered through the whole war, from Fish Creek to Batoche, shouting in pain all day long. My head bled all night.

When I arrived in the States, the wound started to bleed again. I tried to get help to fix it. There was a cut two inches long and three-quarters of an inch deep, right on the top of my head. It was lucky I had a very thick skull or I would have been killed. The doctors told me a main artery had been cut. I had many accidents right after the war. When I turned hard it was like being hit over the head with a hammer, and many times I lost consciousness and fell. But most of the time I would fall and recover right away.

One day in a blacksmith's shop, I fell face-first on top of a pile of angle iron and marked up my whole face.

Since then the accidents haven't happened much, the circulation has no doubt been restored by the nearby arteries growing little by little to replace the cut one.

o o o

I was supposed to have been in France with Buffalo Bill. It is not true! I worked for Buffalo Bill, but only in America, and that was before 1889. During his trip to Europe, Buffalo Bill was going to pass through England and I did not have my amnesty, so I could not go. With Buffalo

Bill in France were Michel Dumas, Ambroise Lepine—brother of old Maxime Lepine, general in the 1870 rebellion, but no part of the "rebellion" of 1885—Jules Marion, son of Edouard Marion, and Maxime Goulet, brother of Roger Goulet—who had died lately at the land bureau in Winnipeg.

Michel Dumas and Ambroise Lepine did not stay long with Buffalo Bill. They were almost always drunk and were shown the door. Lepine pretended that he had been mistaken for Buffalo Bill and that it was jealousy that got him fired.

They were out on the streets, so they went to knock on the door of the Canadian consulate in Paris. That is when Dumas tried to pass for me. M. Pierre Toussin, secretary for the Canadian Consul, was asked to present them to a general who was the mayor of the Commune of Neuilly where Buffalo Bill's show was set up. "General," said Toussin, "I wish to present to you Generals Dumont and Lepine of the Army of the Métis Rebellion in Canada." The General took an interest in them just as he would show good will to any brother-in-arms. It was because of his intervention and the Canadian Consul that Michel Dumas returned to Canada as me, Gabriel Dumont.

Ambroise Lepine was brought back, by the son of Adolphe Ouimet, a Montréal lawyer.

Goulet was also shown the door by Buffalo Bill. His brother sent him the money to come home. Jules Marion, who was hired to drive a dog team, stayed his full time.

I went to France once in 1895 for one year and never left Paris.

I got my amnesty in the winter of 1886, one year after the others.

Napoleon Nault, Gabriel Dumont and [?] Gladue.

Archives of Manitoba (Dumont, Gabriel 4 [N7582]).

Courtesy Saskatoon Public Library Local History Room.

MY STORY

Around 1880 or 1881, the Métis of Batoche and St. Laurent got very tired of having to pay for the wood they cut for planks and firewood.

I led the discontent. I could not understand why this was happening, since it was still wild country. In Manitoba, four or five years after it became a province we could still cut wood on unoccupied land for free. Father Vegreville, who was against this as well, and I, drew up a petition together.

One day I went to find Laferté (Louis Schmidt), and told him we could not take this any more. He told me, "You cannot stop it: the law is passed."

I answered him, "I will try everything." We called a meeting at Batoche. They wanted me to be president but I said no, because I wanted to be able to talk.

So they made Emmanuel Champagne president. I told them again how the governor was not yet the master of our country. "We left Manitoba because we were not free, and we came to this new wild country to be free. And now we have to pay to cut firewood? Where can we go? What can we do? We cannot let this happen. The government has made its first move against us and if we let them get away with it, there will be more laws coming."

The meeting decided to make another petition. Michel Dumas, also known as the Rat, closed his office. He was the agent in charge of seizing the wood. He offered to sign the petition, and at the same time keep right on seizing the wood until a new order came about. I said to him,

"We have no need of your signature. You are exactly who we don't need. We are working against you."

"Oh, Mr. Dumont," said Dumas, "I want to sign to show my sympathy for the rest of you." He kept the petition in his hand until his uncle Isidore took it, and told him, "Listen to what Gabriel says: he does not want you to sign, understand?"

Then I went to find Clarke, who lived at Fort Carlton and was the district representative in the assembly. (Batoche and Alex Cayen were our other two representatives.)

When we arrived at Carlton, we told Clarke the reason for our visit. "We have been forced to pay for wood we cut here in the wilderness. We cannot let that happen. This tax is too much. We have come to you to find a way to stop this, because you are our representative. You must see that this is by right—and if you do not do something about it there will be more to come."

Clarke answered that he could do nothing himself: the law had been passed. All the representatives were there when it was, and they were all in favour of it. "Well," I said, "if it has become a law it must be abolished. I will make you—I will force you—to make the trip. If you won't go, then we do not need a representative."

"No, there is nothing I can do," answered Clarke. "It isn't even worth trying."

"Try it! Here is a paper." I took the petition from my pocket. "Take it with you to Winnipeg. And get going—there is not much time." Clarke looked at the petition with all the signatures and said, "With this, of course I'll go. But you didn't tell me what you had done, Mr. Dumont. I will get to work on this with pleasure because with this I can get you some service, some relief from the chambers where I am the member for this district. I am going to telegraph right away, and if they don't answer me, I will go to Winnipeg at government expense, of course."

In five days he got the answer: an order allowing the Métis of the Saskatchewan to cut wood freely for their own use.

Michel Dumas got the news of this new measure and a few days later met Jean Dumont, whose wood he had seized before, and told him he could have it back. Jean who was cutting wood told him, "It is a good day today, I can cut all I can carry. There was never any doubt when we went to work against you."

This all happened around 1881 or 1882. Around this same time we also saw that the Métis of Edmonton were being pushed off their land by new settlers. When they reported this to the police they were told that nothing could be done. The Métis were the first to live there, and claimed squatters' rights. There were about thirty Métis families who had been forced out, and they decided to get justice for themselves. They accused the government of ignoring their rights to the land, which had been signed over to these new occupants, whom the government represented. They threatened to pull the small houses of the settlement down with their horses and some ropes.

The settlers naturally became very irritated. But the Métis did not leave soon, and came very close to spilling blood.

The Métis of the Saskatchewan learned of their fate and feared that the same might happen to them. The problems we were having with the government and the wood superintendent were not good signs. We did not want to have to fight for our rights, which had been won in the rebellion of 1870. But we were resolved to demand our rights from the government.

During 1882 or 1883 we were greatly occupied with this issue. We had meetings that were my idea, along with Charles Nolin and others, at Batoche, St. Laurent and almost at Prince Albert.

We petitioned the government but never got an answer.

The last meeting in this period was held at the home of my father, Isidore Dumont. He had become discouraged, and only wanted to know how we could quickly and easily obtain our rights. An English Métis named Andrew Spence answered, "There is only one man who can help us now: Riel."

Everyone agreed. Riel was the only one who could intervene between the Métis and the government in 1870, and that negotiation had made those rights a reality.

It was quickly decided to bring Riel back to Saskatchewan to help us draw up petitions, and use his contacts and abilities. We wanted a treaty like the one he had negotiated with the government. (Riel's papers were found by Baptiste Rochelot after the battle. He left them with a priest from Winnipeg named Campeau, who was originally from Montréal and had come to Batoche with Lemieux after the rebellion.)

Jimmie Isbister and I were asked to go and find Riel. The people would look after our families while we were gone. Moise Ouellette and Michel Dumas volunteered to go with us because they wanted to meet Riel and would beg him in case he did not want to come back. Lafontaine and Gardupuy were going to Lewiston to get Lafontaine's mother. They came with us part of the way.

I had a small simple wagon. Moise and Jimmie each had two hitch wagons.

It was my first trip to Montana, but somehow I knew exactly how long it would be to the Mission of St. Pierre. So I said before I left, "The fifteenth day after we leave here, you will know we are getting close."

In fact, we left on the nineteenth of May and on the morning of June 4 we arrived.

Riel was teaching there with the Fathers. It was exactly eight o'clock when we entered the courtyard of the mission. Mass had just begun. We waited in a small house that Jimie Swan lived in. We asked him where Riel was and he told us that Riel was helping with mass, as he did every day. I then spoke to an old woman named Arcand, who said she would go and let Riel know there were some people who wished to speak to him right away.

Riel left the chapel and came toward Swan's house. When I saw him I went out to meet him with my hand outstretched. Riel took my hand and held it in his and said to me, "You are a man who has travelled far. I don't know you, but you seem to know me."

"Yes," I answered, "and I think you might know the name Gabriel Dumont."

"Of course, quite well," answered Riel, "I know it quite well. It is good to see you but, if you will excuse me, I am going to hear the rest of the mass. Please go and wait for me at my home, over there, the house near the small bridge. My wife is there and I will be there shortly."

After returning from mass, Riel asked why we from the Northwest had come to see him and what we wanted.

He seemed surprised and flattered by what he heard. As he answered us I knew that I would always remember his words: "God has helped me understand why you have made this long trip, and since there are four of you who have arrived on the fourth, and you wish to leave with a fifth, I cannot answer today. You must wait until the fifth. I will give you my answer in the morning."

We were in a great hurry—but we could wait one day before leaving. So we would wait until the morning for an answer.

The next day, as he promised, Riel gave his answer: "It has been fifteen years since I gave my heart to my country. I am ready to give it again now, but I cannot leave my little family. If you can arrange for them to come, I will go with you."

"Good," we answered. "With our three wagons we can make room." Riel had his wife, a son about four years old, and a two-year-old daughter. "But," added Riel, "I cannot leave for eight days. I am employed as a teacher here and I would like to make arrangements to leave properly."

We waited, as he asked us to do, and on the eighth day we started our trip. After a few days, we arrived at Benton, Montana. Riel took mass and afterward he went to the priest to ask for his blessing. The priest told him that he didn't see why he should give his blessing.

Nevertheless, since we were stopping for twenty-four hours to rest the horses, the next morning, Riel went to mass again. After mass the priest came to find him and told him, "Yesterday I answered you as I did because I didn't think my blessing would be useful. But since I see you still want it, I will give it to you."

Riel accepted and left to find us because he wanted all of us to receive the priest's blessing. I was the only one who wanted to go to the church for this. Riel also brought his wife and children. All five of us kneeled at the communion table to receive the blessing Riel had asked for.

As soon as we left and were back on the trail, I made up a commemorative prayer for this blessing. It just came out of my mouth: "Father, give me courage, and my belief and my faith in the holy blessing I have received in Your holy name, in order that I will remember it all of my life right up to the hour of my death. Amen."

The twenty-second day after we left the Mission of St. Pierre we arrived at Fish Creek, where sixty Métis had come to meet us. That night we camped at my place, some in the house, the rest nearby in tents. It was the fifth of June 1884.

The next day we left for Batoche. I went ahead to get Father Moulin to prepare the church where Riel was to make a speech. But so many wanted to hear him, when he got there he realized that the church was too small. So he spoke to the crowd that had followed him, outside behind the church. He spoke of rights, treaties and other matters.

Riel stayed first at Moise Ouellette's. Then he went to Charles Nolin's with his family and stayed there until the rebellion.

The summer and winter passed, and during this time many meetings and petitions were made. (I don't remember whether Riel ever talked about buying the *Prince Albert Journal*, as Caron reported.)

One of the last meetings was held at Joseph Halcrow's in February of 1885.

None of the old petitions, all addressed to the government in Ottawa, were ever answered.

In the end, Riel and the other leaders of the movement were losing patience, and one day he let the words slip: "They should at least answer us, either yes or no. And they cannot say no, since we are only asking for what has already been promised. If they don't give us our rights we will have to rebel again."

After that the word rebellion was on the tongue of every Métis, along with the tragic meaning it would soon acquire. We all remembered the rebellion of 1870, which had been very peaceful for the most part—there had been only one victim. Scott got what he deserved for his extreme fanaticism. This time the Métis who were talking about rebellion felt that a noisy threat would bring them their rights. These were the memories that were held in everyone's minds.

No people in the world are as strong and good as the Métis, but still given a choice between war and their rights, many would rather give up their rights than fight.

But then there was still Clarke, chief factor of Fort Carlton, who had returned from Winnipeg by way of Qu'Appelle. When he passed through Batoche he asked those who were there, "Have you had more meetings? What have you been doing all this time? Did you get your answer?"

Then Clarke told them, "Good, good—it won't be long now. There are eighty policemen coming. I saw them at Humboldt, and tomorrow or the next day Riel and Dumont will be taken."

Naturally everyone was excited.

The next afternoon we had a general meeting at the church. Riel and I addressed the crowd. I told the crowd the latest news: "The police are coming to take Riel." I also asked the people, "What are you going to do? Here is a man who has done so much for us. Are we going to let him slide through our hands? Let us make a plan."

Riel then spoke: "We send petitions, they send police to take us— Gabriel Dumont and me. But I know very well how this works. It is I who have done wrong. The government hates me because I have already made them give in once. This time they will give up nothing. I also think it would be better for me to go now. I must leave you and I feel I should go now. Once I am gone you may be able to get what you want more easily. Yes—I really think that it would be better if I went back to Montana."

The whole crowd interrupted and told him, "No, we won't let you go. You have worked hard for our rights and you can't quit now."

"Then," said Riel, "if I must, I will desert."

"If you desert, we will desert with you."

I answered them: "It is for the best that we go and cross the line. We will not be insulted and made prisoners."

"We won't let that happen. Don't be afraid of that," answered the crowd.

"So what will you do?"

"When they come, we will take up arms and no one will lay a hand on you!"

"What are you saying?" I asked. "You talk of taking up arms. But what arms do you have to battle the government? And how many of you are there?"

"Yes!" They answered as one. "We will take up arms if you want us to." Riel would not say whether he would stay.

So I continued: "'Yes,' you say. I know you well, I know all of you like my children. I know how much you are all for taking up arms. It is good to be firm, but not everyone is. So I ask again, how many will take up arms? All in favour of taking up arms, raise your hands."

Instead of raising their hands, the whole stood up as one. There were cries of joy and they yelled, "If we are to die for our country, we will die together."

I was frozen. Even though I was the most enthusiastic one there and capable of any heroism in the face of danger, I tried to remain calm and take judgment into account. I said again, "I can see that you have made your decision, but I wonder if you will become tired and discouraged. Me—I will never give up, but how many will be there with me? Two or three?"

"We will be with you, right to the end!" answered the whole crowd.

"Good then," I said. "This is good. If you really want to take up arms, I will lead you as I always have."

"Good then. If you will lead us, that is good—to arms, to arms."

It was done. The armed rebellion had begun. Without the news that Clarke had reported—that the police were coming to take Riel—no one ever dreamed that a military insurgence would come again. Now it was here. In any case, we had tried all peaceful means to obtain our rights.

It was Clarke who put fire to the powder by reporting the news. The news was false. It was invented to scare off the organizers of the meetings.

Thirty men went to get their guns and then returned. After we had decided to take up arms, we left the church and went toward Norbert Delorme's house (now Laderoute's). The crowd stayed there with me while Riel and Napoleon Nault toured up to the edge of Fish Creek.

Then I said, "Now when I see a government man, I will take him prisoner. You may think I am going too far, but no. The moment we took up arms, we were in rebellion, and this is not too much."

Right at that moment, the Indian agent arrived with his man, coming from the reserve. "I am taking you prisoner," I told him.

"Oh. Why?"

"We have taken up arms against the government and we are going to take all those who work for the government prisoners."

"That's good," said the agent. "Take us."

Sometime after, we heard a cart coming up the trail. I saw Jardine and went down the path to arrest him. He whipped his horse. "Stop!" I yelled.

Jardine pushed his horse.

"Stop!" I yelled again. Jardine whipped his horse again.

"If you don't stop, I will shoot your horse!" I yelled, putting my hand on my rifle.

This time Jardine stopped. "Where are you going?" I asked.

"It's none of your business where I'm going."

"There will be no problem if you tell the truth about your trip, but this is no honest trip. You are going to Duck Lake to report what has happened, and I am making you prisoner."

"But my horse, and the one I am leading?"

"Your horse is also a prisoner."

"But I am looking for medicine for my wife who is sick. I am trying to take it to her."

"Give it to me," I said. "I will get it to her." I took the medicine and Jardine stayed prisoner.

While this was happening Riel returned and wanted to know what had happened since he had left.

I told him we had already taken three prisoners.

"Yes! Yes, that's good," said Riel

Then we headed back toward the church and stopped at Jarreau's house where we stayed a while.

That evening, the eighteenth of March, we raided Baker's store.

That same evening we also arrested two men who were trying to repair the telegraph. They were taken by captains Isidore Dumont, Augustin Laframboise, and their men.

I stayed at Batoche. When they crossed the river with their two prisoners, I went out to meet them. "Have you disarmed them?" I asked.

And when they answered no, I said, "Oh well, you have done your duty as captains."

So I searched them myself, but they didn't have any guns.

The Peace Mission of Mitchell and Tom MacKay

Mitchell and Tom MacKay came to Jarreau's house to try and calm our spirits.

Tom MacKay accused Riel of being the cause of all the trouble. "As for Gabriel," he said, "I think he doesn't understand what is happening. He has made a mistake."

I answered, "Tom, you may be mistaken. I have not been told what to do. When someone tells me something, I understand. I am not mistaken, like you. You have gone against us, and yet you are a Métis and have the same rights to gain as we do. I don't know if you have even a small spoonful of good sense. Your blood is all water. If it wasn't for your friend, I would take you prisoner." Mitchell had no answer.

It was finally decided that Riel would send two men to accompany these two back to the police coming from Carlton in order to deliver a message. The two men sent by Riel were Nolin and Max Lepine. They went with them to the police, but the papers were never delivered and we never found out why.

The Pillage of Mitchell's Store, March 24

It was reported that Mitchell had said, "If they want to come and take my guns, I will fight them with a pitchfork."

At this time I told Riel, "You have given them all the advantages. They are coming to Duck Lake: we could catch them crossing the lake. And while we're there, why don't we take Mitchell's store? We have taken up arms, yet we just sit here. If we wanted to move now, we could catch them by surprise."

"But," said Riel, "it won't be easy. They won't just let us get away with it."

"Give me ten men and put me in charge."

Riel agreed, and I chose ten men and set out. I chose from the committed: Edouard Dumont, Phillippe Gardupuy, Baptiste Deschamps, Baptiste Arcand, Baptiste Ouellette, Norbert Delorme, Joseph Delorme, and Augustin Laframboise.

We left Batoche an hour after noon. Mitchell knew we were coming, so when we arrived the store was closed. An English Métis named Magnus Burnstein, a farmer from Duck Lake, was found nearby. He was also a clerk in the store, and he told me it was locked.

"Fine, fine," I said. "We'll break down the doors." And I went to do it.

"Well," said Burnstein, "they left me the keys: here they are."

We went in the store but all the guns had disappeared. We did find some lead shot in the latrine ditch. We stayed a moment, and then we were told somebody was coming.

Soon after, Riel arrived with all the men from Batoche.

When they got there I sent my ten men to go and watch the Carlton Trail—I didn't trust that the police wouldn't try a surprise attack. We crossed Duck Lake on the ice, stopped at the reserve, and looked after our horses until nightfall. Then I chose two of my men, Baptiste Arcand and Baptiste Ouellette, to go and watch the road. Before long they returned to say they had seen two policemen.

I took my brother Edouard, Baptiste Deschamps, Phillippe Gardupuy and an Indian who wanted to go along, and left the others at the reserve. We went to find the two policemen who had been spotted. I took a Canadien Grey.

"If they try to defend themselves," I said, "we will kill them. If not, we will not harm them."

We left at a gallop by the light of the moon. We talked under our breath as we returned to the exact spot where they had seen the police. Then on the big bluff at the edge of the woods, we saw the two policemen riding side by side. We moved toward them under cover. When we got to the top of the bluff we were at a good distance to start our charge, and I yelled, "Go—turn your horses loose! Get them!"

There was a hard crust on the snow and it was impossible to go off the path. I had the best horse and was trying to catch up to the horsemen, but decided to wait for the rest to reach the top of the hill, to give the horses good footing. When all the horses had arrived we were still right behind the policemen, as I had hoped. I was still mounted and came up on the left side of the two and said to them, "Stop! If you try to escape I will kill you."

"Why?" asked the rider. "I am a surveyor."

"What are you trying to tell me?" I answered. "There is nothing to survey out here at this time of night." At the same time I passed my leg across the neck of my horse and grabbed the policeman by the arms, pulled him off his horse, and fell to the ground with him.

Phillippe Gardupuy and Baptiste Deschamps went after the other policeman. Because I had made my move first, the road was blocked and they couldn't catch up to him right away. So Baptiste Deschamps yelled, "Stop or I'll kill you!" There can be no doubt the policeman heard him and understood. He turned around to look back, and right then the movement of his hands changed the footing of his horse. The horse suddenly stumbled, and the policeman fell off. Phillippe Gardupuy passed on my right and went to arrest him. Baptiste Deschamps was already on top of him and, without stopping completely, jumped to the ground and seized the policeman by the arms. Gardupuy arrived at the same time to help.

I had disarmed my prisoner and went to disarm the other one, saying, "You are my prisoners, and I am taking you to Duck Lake." The policemen asked for their horses. "You can use these others, but we will not give you back your own." I chose the worst and gave them each one, but the policemen preferred to walk.

When we arrived back at Mitchell's store, the policemen asked for Sheriff Ross.

"He isn't sheriff tonight," I laughed. "I have taken him prisoner. He is under guard with the other prisoners at Batoche." We went right back out to watch the Carlton Trail. We went to the same spot but saw nothing more. When day came we thought the police wouldn't risk sending any more scouts, so we retired. We got back to Duck Lake and had just put our horses in the stable, when we heard the cry: "Here come the police!"

In fact it was three policemen who were scouting up to Duck Lake. Quickly we found horses to go after them, and some had already left before I got my horse saddled. I wanted to be at the front so I strained to catch them, but instead of following the path, I picked my way over the snow. I trusted my horse, but we got caught in deep drifts and lost more time. I was a quarter mile behind Jim Short and Patrice Fleury.

As they chased them, the three policemen were joined by Tom MacKay who told them, "Quickly—save yourselves! Because Gabriel is going to take this whole unit prisoner, just like the other two."

Edouard Dumont had joined Fleury and Short in chasing the three Mounted Police almost back to the troop. There were twenty sleighs. One had been stopped and turned sideways to prepare a defense against our attack. As they approached, a policeman yelled from one of the sleighs, "Stop, or we'll kill you!"

They stopped but stayed on their horses. When I arrived behind them I said to them, "What are you doing? Why are you still on your horses? You can see they are going to kill you. Get off your horses and get ready to defend yourselves." I got off my horse and chased it away with a slap on the neck. I took my carbine and advanced toward the police to harass them. When we were about twenty-five yards away, a sergeant in the second sleigh yelled, "If you don't stop, I will kill you!" Just then he saw me with my carbine. "Don't try it," I yelled at him. "I will kill you first." I shouldered my gun and aimed it at the sergeant. He put his rifle across his knees, and I moved up so I was about fifteen yards away.

In two or three jumps, I was at the sleigh and on top of the sergeant who had time to lift his rifle. I hit him in the chest with the barrel of my rifle, and he fell back in the sleigh, his rifle pointed straight up in the air. Because he had gloves on, it went off by mistake. The sergeant got back up in the sleigh and threatened me with his rifle. "Don't even move, or I will kill you."

Tom MacKay, on horseback a short distance away, yelled to me, "Look out: if you don't stop, it'll be the end for you." I answered him, "You watch out. This is all your fault, all of it. You brought the police and whatever happens will be your responsibility. Don't you realize there are Canadian Métis fighting to the death with us?" As MacKay answered, I lifted my rifle to take a swing at him. He tried to turn his horse, but this put his hind legs off the path, on the high side, and he sank deeply in the snow. The rider was now lower and I had a better chance to hit him. I swung, but the horse made a quick movement and stopped at an opening in the trail. The end of the rifle slid over

MacKay's back. He spurred his horse, and shot forward. I took another swing, but only got the horse on the buttocks.

A policeman in another sleigh took aim at me and was going to kill me. But when I took aim, he put his gun across his knees. At the same time all the sleighs started. Jim Short and Patrice Fleury stayed on horseback at a distance. Only Edouard Dumont, at my urging, had gotten off his horse and advanced toward them while I was talking this war-like way. As the sleighs were starting to move, Edouard ran to the first and tried to climb on by grabbing the harness. He wanted to take the whole convoy prisoner. They pushed him back and he tumbled into the snow. All the sleighs left at a gallop in the direction of Carlton.

Jim Short was yelling insults after them, but I said to him, "What are you trying to do! You didn't even get off your horse and now that they are gone you fire off your silliness. If that is all you are going to do, you will be well-rested and your feet will stay warm."

We returned to Duck Lake, and the others who arrived at the end turned back as well.

We put our horses in the stable again and sat down to eat. We had just finished when we heard the police were coming again.

We all left to go and waited at the big hill just off the side.

We met a party of scouts, and followed them. They made it back to the main troop.

While we were going after them I told my brother Isidore, "I don't want to start killing them, I want to take prisoners. If they try to kill us then we will kill them."

When we got to the police I saw that all the sleighs were off the path. There was no pattern, but they were well-placed for battle. Not far off the trail there was a small, low foundation. I didn't even slow down, but left the trail and was soon at the wall with my men. Twenty-five jumped from their horses and went on the defensive.

Crozier himself came forward. Isidore Dumont and an Indian went out to meet him. Crozier and the Indian, who was unarmed, put out their hands. Then a policeman and an English Métis named McKay moved his horse forward a step, and the Indian jumped him and tried to take his rifle. It didn't work. Most thought that the Indian who was killed by the policeman was the first victim of the war. But I think it might have been Isidore who was killed first. The Indian was unarmed and my brother had his rifle, and the policeman had to kill the armed man first so he would not be killed by him. Even if the policeman had killed the Indian first, I had no doubt that my brother had been killed right after. He was killed without firing his gun—we found it by his side.

Edouard Dumont said that after the first shot he saw the Indian still standing, trying to return. And although he hadn't seen the exact moment he had fallen, he was not the victim of the first shot.

This Indian was the godson of Charles Trottier. He did not die quickly, not until we arrived at Duck Lake.

After the first shot I ordered my men to get up and fire. This fight lasted twenty minutes.

Riel was in the small hollow with us. He was on his horse, a crucifix in his hand, held up in the air. He would not get down from his horse. He was very exposed—the small hollow was not deep enough for a mounted man to be in cover. As we began to turn the enemy, one of them gave the signal to depart. I was hidden behind a small bluff, and I saw a sleigh cross an opening in the trees. I told my men I would give them trouble when they tried to climb in the sleigh. When a policeman showed his face, a bullet in the head made him fall back in the sleigh.

Then I yelled to my men: "Courage. Follow me. I am going to board the sleighs, hear me?"

Just as I came upon the enemy who were firing right at me, I fell, seated on the snow. A bullet creased the top of my head making a furrow, and the ricochet whistled away. Blood spurted into the air. Delorme yelled to me, "Oh no—they got you!" But I answered him, "When you don't lose your head, you're not dead." At the same time I told Baptiste Vandal, "Cousin, take my rifle!" Vandal left his old rifle there and took my fourteen-shot repeater. "Good—take my cartridges too." Vandal unhooked my belt, "No, not that one," I said. "Undo the other one."

I then tried to get up to my knees, but it was my gun belt that held up my pants. Vandal didn't do it up and my pants fell down.

My brother Edouard had been over by the edge of a small ravine, and he slid and pulled himself over to me and dragged me to cover.

Augustin Laframboise was stretched out nearby. He had dragged himself there and tried to get to his knees to make the sign, but he fell again on his side. I said to him, "Do not be afraid. Soon you will be all right." But Laframboise was already dead: a bullet had passed through his chest.

By then the English were completely in flight. Edouard Dumont shouted, "After them! Exterminate them!" But Riel, always with his crucifix in hand, said, "We have had enough of that. Let them go."

They put me on my horse and tied my head with handkerchiefs. When I passed my brother Isidore, I got down, but I could only confirm that he was dead.

A little farther on I was told, "Behind that bluff there is a young volunteer, wounded in the leg." I went around the fence and came up to him: I was going to finish him off. I told him it would be quick and painless. I reached for my revolver, but it was right in the middle of my back and I couldn't reach it from the left or the right. While I was trying to get my gun, Riel arrived and stopped me from killing him. You may ask why I wanted to kill the wounded. They came to fight against us and I was shocked at the way my brother was killed and that they had shaved me.

We cared for their wounded with ours.

We returned to Duck Lake before noon. Riel gave a speech at once. "The world rained blood," he said. "You deserve congratulations as does your leader, Mr. Dumont. Let us give him three cheers." They saluted me with cheers.

The English had left many of their dead on the field, so Riel told them they could come and recover them.

He sent an envoy, a prisoner taken at Humboldt, with a letter from Riel and me, giving our promise that there was no risk. We gave the prisoner a buggy and a horse to take him to Carlton.

He delivered the letter, but the English thought it was a trap. Better yet—they accused the prisoner of being an accomplice in the ambush and made him a prisoner in the fort.

I wanted to go to the Pinery, and stop the police. But Riel was against that, saying it was too savage to go and attack them at night. I was very

Gabriel Dumont with his rifle "Le Petit."
Glenbow Archives, Calgary (NA-3432-2).

upset by Riel's opposition, and told him, "If you are going to give them the advantage like that, we cannot win."

The Métis, who were near the fire at Fort Carlton, saved part of the spoils.

St. Denis told me, "If you want to come to the Pinery, we can destroy them." But I was very tired. I had to sleep on the march: it was my second night without sleep.

When the police got back to Prince Albert, the prisoner who had taken the letter from Riel protested his innocence again. This time they believed him and set him free. The day after the fighting, the bodies were still laying in the sun. Riel sent two sleighs, and the men carried the bodies into one of the two small houses near the battlefield.

The next day three sleighs arrived from Prince Albert to take the dead. Jackson, the brother of Riel's secretary, and the prisoner were with them. The police came almost to Duck Lake, where they unharnessed and cared for their horses. There were nine dead bodies. Jackson's brother stayed with us: the secretary had already gone mad.

The total number of Métis fighters was about two hundred, including Indians, but they weren't all armed, especially the Indians. Many had not much more than sticks. There was one who was armed with a staff, with a curved top, used to dig potatoes. The Sioux of Saskatoon or Round Prairie had not come yet. Some came before Fish Creek, and the rest came before Batoche.

In that little valley and the two houses, there had been about twenty-five fighters. They didn't fire much, but they took an effective part in a short fight.

It was during the Battle of Duck Lake that Nolin ran away. He hadn't gone over to the enemy when the cry, "Here come the police!" came. When he heard the rifle shots he went wild with terror. He took a small white pony belonging to Belanger's son and ran just like we knew he would, just like a fox.

He had been in at the beginning of the rebellion and had always been one with the Métis. He made this tragic choice because he was afraid for his safety, and began to question our plans. I decided to execute him. It happened sometime between the declaration of the rebellion and Duck Lake. I sent three men to find him, but he had fled to the priest's house at St. Laurent Mission.

We returned to Batoche the following day and called a meeting at G. Fisher's house. I was staying at Batoche's house. Only his mother and children were there. Eugene Boucher (a store clerk), his son-in-law (who later became a deputy), Batoche's brother Isidore, Baptiste Boyer and Fisher were gone.

It was also then that we brought all the families to Batoche. We fed all the animals that the Sioux and Métis had rounded up from near the English Métis settlements. Some had made common cause with us from the start, but had stopped marching with us, so we treated them as enemies. We treated the animals taken in the rebellion exactly the same way.

Riel, Isidore, the Indian and I were on horseback. I had thought that Isidore had been killed on his horse, but now I doubt it. The Indian was killed while on foot, since he had left his little pony behind. I was in the hollow fifty or sixty yards from the Indian and Isidore. We knew that the police were from Carlton, but we had no idea they were going to attack. Riel had come to Duck Lake because he was afraid to stay at Batoche alone.

We heard about the fire at Fort Carlton the next morning.

Jackson's brother was staying with us, with our permission, to visit his brother. He was helping to care for the wounded and the police we had taken prisoner at Duck Lake.

Hilaire Paternotre had wintered near Fort Carlton, and stayed for a while after the battle. He put out the fire at the fort.

Fish Creek

At the news of Middleton's arrival, Riel wanted to stay and defend Batoche, but my plan was to go out and meet the enemy, because they were already showing weakness by hesitating to advance. Besides, we had nothing to lose.

This time we followed my plan and on the twenty-third we left to meet Middleton. Riel and I had about 150 men with us. We left Edouard Dumont at Batoche to guard the prisoners.

We followed the trail along the bank of the river, some on horses, others on foot. There were Métis, Sioux and Cree.

Riel kept making us stop so he could say the rosary.

About four miles past the coulee at Roger Goulet's, we stopped to eat. It was midnight, and we killed and ate two animals. When we finished, Emmanuel Champagne and Moise Carrière arrived, sent by Edouard, who wanted the help of thirty men led by either Riel or me: a troop of police had been spotted on the trail from Qu'Appelle.

I refused to turn back, and even though Riel himself had not been asked, he offered. Most of the fighters had left Batoche with some regret, wanting to protect their families.

Riel wanted to take fifty men. There would be blood everywhere, so I chose the men who would return, and stayed with one hundred.

We marched on. "This time," I said, "we won't be saying rosary so much, so we'll move faster." We were almost to McIntoche's, and it was almost daylight. The Sioux came to me and said they would not attack the government by day, and they would not be forced. They wanted to return.

My plan had been to surprise the enemy camp during the night, to spring a prairie fire on them, take advantage of their confusion, and massacre them. If we had found the English camp that first night, Middleton's soldiers would have been lucky to get out alive.

I decided to go back and wait for the enemy at Fish Creek coulee. Ignace Poitras, also known as Betillet, had a good runner and said to me, "Take my horse and go find out where they are." One of the Touronds had a good horse and gave it to Napoleon Nault. We went together to scout the enemy.

I ordered the men not to use the trail, to leave no signs for the enemy by staying on the prairie. They paid little attention to my orders, and when I returned they had made many fires right on the path.

Napoleon Nault and I got to within a half-mile of the English camp. I thought we might meet a scout, and I was afraid that Nault might try and capture him. I wanted to get behind them, kill them and take their guns. That was always my first thought: to get more guns.

We scouted the prairie around their camp without seeing a single scout, so we returned to join the men at Fish Creek. It was early in the day. Since it was their place, the Touronds gave us an animal that we ate along the way.

I was constantly sending out scouts. Gabriel Bertrand brought the news that the enemy was near, just as we finished breakfast. It was the thirty scouts. I placed my men on the bluff and moved forward with twenty horsemen. I ordered my men to let the first of the enemy come all the way down to the creek and only then fire from above, when they were all strung out along the trail near the bluff. If any were left behind, my horsemen would cut them down and take their arms.

But the advance guard of the enemy saw tracks on the trail and returned to the troop.

The English finally found us when some of the scouts broke away. One of them advanced almost to our lines. "Let them come," I said, "and when enough of them get close we will get them."

But they would not come any closer; there wasn't even a good chance to fire a shot. I wanted to slaughter them and get their guns. A group of horsemen charged the scouts. Horses were everywhere and I was cut off again and again, but finally I caught up to the scouts. I was about fifteen yards away when I heard someone behind yell, "There they are—the police." I got off two shots, but none fell. They got to a small bluff and took cover there.

Meanwhile, I noticed the English soldiers moving through the trees. I stopped my horse and turned around in the middle of the nearest trees, and made my way along the bluff, to stay concealed from the enemy as long as possible. I got back to my men without taking another shot.

I got off my horse and tied it behind the bluff. I went with a young Cree from bluff to bluff to look for the enemy and get an idea of their numbers. When we arrived at the bluff where I had shot at the scouts, we found a horse with no rider. He had no doubt been knocked off among the trees. It wasn't long before we found the enemy—they were very close. We fired our guns in the direction of the English, and flattened ourselves to the ground.

They couldn't tell who had fired the shots or where they came from, so we fired again. This time they saw the smoke and returned fire.

We retreated, and when we arrived at the coulee, we found a Sioux who told us one of his people had been killed, and most of the Métis had run off.

I saw Ignace Poitras leading a horse. I followed him a short way and found the runaways. The eight Métis and seven Sioux had gotten about a quarter of a mile. I took them to a coulee east of the bluff where the attack had started, and there were already forty-five Métis.

Some of the Métis with me were Antoine Lafontaine, Pierre Sansregret, Edouard Dumont—son of an Assiniboine Métis raised by my Uncle—J.B. Trottier, W. Trottier, young Ladouceur, who had no gun but was carrying instead a flag of the virgin, and two young Indians.

The seven Sioux fought about fifteen yards from our nine Métis. I had my fourteen-shot repeater, and the young men were giving me their guns to shoot. When we got down to our last seven bullets, I said, "We are going to start a fire line in front of the police." The wind was blowing toward the enemy. We started the fire, and as I was walking the right line to make sure the fire was going, I saw the problem. I told my men, "We are going to make a sweep, yelling and screaming. March right behind the flames." I always stayed right behind the biggest flames, and when we were about forty yards from the police the fire went out. It was at the edge of a small wet woods. The police were in flight. As we advanced, we found many dead, and no doubt there were many more dead in the underbrush because the water in the little creek was red. We didn't find any rifles or cartridges. The sun had gone down.

The English front-line had no doubt already rejoined the troops who were battling the forty-five. "Now that they are a unit," I said, "I am going to get behind them so we can save the forty-five." I wanted to go immediately and scout. But the Sioux refused to follow, so I went alone. I took my horse, which had been tied in the bottom of the coulee. I got almost to the edge of the coulee where the enemy was hidden, close to the forty-five. They saw me and fired on me, so I fell back and joined my men.

We went to Calixte Tourond's house to eat. We found all we needed, and killed some chickens and roasted them.

Isidore Parenteau arrived with a buggy, two Sioux, and a half-barrel of powder. Soon after, two more Sioux arrived on horseback, then Phillippe Gardupuy and Moise Ouellette. They had left when the men making noise behind the fire line were fired on. The Sioux were scouts.

Edouard Dumont and Baptiste Boucher came and said eighty horsemen were following them.

Snow had fallen and gotten their guns wet, so they had gone to Calixte Lafontaine's to dry them. They would be able to shoot better with dry weapons. I told them not to take poor shots, there would be chances for good shots. We moved toward the coulee, and when we got near I went ahead alone. At the edge of the coulee I found two unsaddled Métis horses, saddled them, and returned to give them to my men. I made them scatter, and told them to attack while yelling and shouting. I went down to old Tourond's house, and got back to the Métis without firing a shot.

The English were in flight. Even the doctor had abandoned all his bandages and medicines. We found almost two bottles of brandy, which we drank to his health. We decided to start a fire at Tourond's and tend to our wounds. Again we didn't fire at the retreating English: my head wound had reopened and I was just too fatigued to follow them.

Riel stayed at Batoche, and passed the time saying the rosary for the fighters as he listened to the rifle shots. At the end, my brother Edouard said, "I want to go and help them. In our family you never hear rifle shots without there being danger, and I can't stay here and leave them to shoot it out."

The wounded were: Challius (also called Charles Thomas) and Charles Carrière, both in the arm; a young Indian, in the hand; Boyer, in the chest—he died; Cardinal, in the neck—he also died; and Pierre Tourond, in the thigh.

Challius was bothered by his arm wound. People say he would never again show his hand.

Return to Batoche

Riel had sent many wagons to Fish Creek that night. I gave orders to the men on foot to return to Batoche quickly. I stayed on horseback to escort the wagons of wounded. I had already seen four or five mounted men leaving.

But I was bleeding from my head wound and suffering terribly. I was still at Tourond's when I said, "I wish I was well enough to do it myself, but I want the rest of you to stay with the wagons, I'll make it on my own."

After going only half a mile, I saw young Jean Dumont and André Letendre. I asked, "Where are you going? I told you to stay with the wounded. You can see I am not well, but if you leave I will have to return." They went back and I went on.

Soon I caught up with the four or five who had deserted earlier. Among them was Napoleon Nault. I was angry with them for leaving. They explained they had left before that order had been given, so they didn't know. I told them I was bleeding a lot and suffering badly, so Napoleon Nault tore a piece of his saddle blanket and bandaged my head.

They helped me back to Batoche. We arrived during the night. Someone stabled my horse and I went to sleep at Batoche's house. But Riel called on me to make my report.

Then I couldn't sleep. I didn't want my men to desert.

Batoche

The English were camped at my homestead. They burned my house and tore down my stables to reinforce the *Northcote* and protect it from gunfire. The Métis scouts saw them and we knew that the *Northcote* was going to come downriver to surround us.

On Saturday they arrived at Batoche before noon. I had placed some Métis on the right side of the river, below the cemetery where the river channel passed a long beach. I thought the *Northcote* would pass close to the side of the river and almost touch the shore. I had also placed, on the other side of the river, some Métis who could fire on the *Northcote*, right after it had been fired on from the left. It would be very difficult to get past these two.

I had also given the order to lower the ferry cable, but the men thought it was low enough and didn't move it.

The cable barely touched the steamboat. It drifted by. The steamboat anchored a little below Fagnan's.

While this was happening, the English had arrived at Caron's. They were trying to turn by Belle Prairie.

I sent Michel Dumas and his men to stop the English from fixing the steamboat's chimney, but they were stopped on the height of the bank and their mission was useless.

During the first push, the English tried to sweep through Belle Prairie. They established a machine gun just this side. Once they fired on me and my horse, from about one mile, but the bullets fell in front of me.

They pulled back at night.

We dug holes near the riverbank, the cemetery and Emmanuel Champagne's. They were about seventy-five yards apart, two or three men in each hole. There were about fifty men in these pits. The other men were hiding among the bush. There were about 150 men on this side of the river, and one hundred on the other side.

At night we fired at the English, as they ate, from the ridge in front of the old forge.

During the night we watched the troops, and the Indians liked to fire on them.

The second day, Middleton worked to establish his fortifications all around his camp so he could sleep easily.

The English started firing right after breakfast. They controlled the church and the cemetery. They moved the machine gun to the small prairie at the top of the trail that ran down into Batoche. It was to the left of the old abandoned trail and to the right of the new trail.

I moved up with my men, crawling along in the small aspens. I told my men, "Let me go ahead. I have already been close enough to take a shot in the head—this time they might not miss. When I start shooting, we must take the machine gun, and get down the trail as quickly as possible." I was almost at the place where I could get a good shot away, when my men began to fire. The artillery hadn't started firing yet and reinforcements were arriving, so I withdrew.

During the first three days, the English could not break our lines of defence. They sat and didn't move much. One report said that Middleton planned to make us use up our bullets, no doubt on the advice of Father Vegreville.

During the last two days, a Sioux named Joli Corbeau broke his leg at the cemetery. J.B. Boucher, the father, was wounded in the buttock.

Armiel Gariepy's wrist was broken and his chest was pierced by the same bullet.

Each night the police returned to their camp, and often there were bullets left on the ground, usually at the foot of a tree, where they had stopped to reload. Often we found machine gun belts which held forty bullets each. These were the same calibre as many of the Métis twelve-shot hunting rifles.

We also took the guns of the dead. We had sixty or seventy at the end.

We also came across something very serious—I was amazed when I was shown the exploding balls. We thought it was understood between nations that only mortars could be explosive, as their debris was very destructive. But for a man in combat to be exposed to exploding bullets was to cause a terrible wound and certain death, which was against the basic principles of war. You wanted to score a direct hit, and temporarily disable, but not necessarily kill, the enemy soldiers. A simple bullet wound would disable a man and his wound would get better, while the wound of an exploding ball caused internal wounds and broke bones, and was always deadly. The government troops committed a huge crime against humanity and against the rights of the men of the Métis nation.

The Fourth Day

Around three o'clock, the English still hadn't moved past where they had been the day before. The sun was already low when they took Batoche's house. They were pushing in on all sides at once, when they stormed through our front-line, they advanced right to the house without stopping.

I was against digging the pits because I knew what was coming. In them the men could stay completely secure and hold on right to the end, and then they couldn't leave without being killed.

This is how it happened. The English advanced in large battalions, without stopping. They rained bullets on the foxholes: the Métis could not raise their heads to fire. When the English got so close that there was no hope, the Métis tried to fire but were killed instantly.

After the English had entered Batoche's house, which was no longer occupied by the Métis, I continued to resist around there for another half hour. With me were the elder Joseph Vandal, and his nephew Joseph Vandal, the elder Ouellette, Pierre Sansregret, David Tourond and a young Sioux.

We were under Batoche's house. Daniel Ross was wounded in Batoche's house: he yelled to me and the others to come and drag him off the field of battle.

"Are you dead or alive?" I yelled to him.

"I won't last much longer," answered Ross.

"I'll be killed if I try. There'll be two deaths instead of one."

Daniel Ross was between Batoche's house and Fisher's store.

The English occupied Batoche's house. There was a red curtain in the upstairs window—we couldn't see them. I kept firing at the curtain to frighten the English, so they would not have time to shoot.

This is when Captain French was shot in the bedroom I had used. He wasn't killed point-blank, but was hit in the bedroom just off the passage, and rolled down the stairs, leaving blood stains. He was found at the bottom of the stairs.

Joseph Vandal, the elder, was also wounded at this point. He had both arms broken, one in two places. He was limping, lost his balance, and fell forward. He tried to get up but failed, so I helped him and said, "Get out of here. Leave now."

"No," said Vandal. "I prefer to die now that I have two broken arms."

"Go! Go!" I told him, but he wouldn't go, and I wouldn't leave him. So I forced him to leave. He went across the trail that went down to the crossing, and I went back to fight from below Batoche's.

A little later we also crossed the trail. The English had already occupied Fisher's store. We fought them from the hill between Fisher's store and his home. It was here that old Ouellette was killed. We were above the women's tents, which had been abandoned. I found Joseph Vandal in Tourond's tent and made him run on alone now. We found him a quarter mile further on, towards Emmanuel Champagne's house, dead and bayonetted.

There was a young wounded Sioux in a wagon near mother Tourond's tent. There was a bullet lodged in his chest: he could not go on. I had to leave him: he was too close to death, bleeding from the mouth. He was the son of Joli Corbeau, who had already been wounded.

After old Ouellette was killed, we returned to the women's tents to wait for the English to come. "It is over," I said. "But only now that we have held up the English long enough for everyone to escape." I was with Joseph Vandal, Pierre Sansregret and David Tourond. We met Phillippe Gariepy, John Ross, Carbatte—the son of John Ross, a young English Métis who was the son of Tom Anderson—Hilaire Paternotre and Henry Smith.

Most wanted to leave, but I wanted us to take our last shots. We followed the English in the half-light, and found many bullets as we went.

We followed the river almost to Emmanuel Champagne's. When we got there, I asked Hilaire Paternotre what he had done with the half-barrel of powder he had found. It was nearby. I wanted him to go and get it, but he wouldn't. So I said to Henry Smith, "You are not afraid, you go and get it. There is no danger. The English aren't there now."

Henry Smith took off his shoes so he could run better. His shoes were hard to run in. He also gave his rifle to John Ross. I waited with his shoes, and the others left. John Ross took his rifle it was gone when Henry returned.

It was night and we needed to eat. I remembered a Sioux lodge nearby that had had a lot of meat in the last few days. I went and got a leg of dried meat.

I came up just this side of Edouard Dumont's where the women had gathered. I gave the calf leg to my wife and told her to share it with the others. Riel's wife was there and so was Riel. It was the last time that I saw him. I heard him say to Madame Riel, "I believe God wants me to live." Everyone was telling them to flee. I wanted to get him a horse so he could get away, if he wanted to. I said to my wife, "Wait for me here." I went to Emmanuel Champagne's stable where I knew there were always horses, but the police had already occupied it. I left without firing on them. I wanted to, but I also wanted to return to my wife and the others.

When I returned she was alone, so I hid her on an island in the river. I went and found a stallion of Batoche's, but he roared and reared so much that I had to tie him in a bluff and go and find another. I met Henry Smith and John Ross' son, who was looking for his father, and Smith wanted his gun back. They told me that Pierriche Parenteau's horses were nearby, so we went to find them.

I found a kettle and carried it with me. Henry Smith had the stallion that had gotten loose. We went to Daniel Gariepy's house, where Maxime Lepine had been living. His closest neighbour was Edouard Dumont. We lit a lamp, and I brought out two plates, two pots and two knives and forks. Then left to get my wife.

I found a young tan mare that had been taken from the police.

When I got near my wife's hiding place, I tied the stallion and the mare in a bluff nearby. While I was tying the stallion, Pierriche Parenteau's horses galloped by. I thought it was the police. It was now the middle of the night. I went to hide near the bluff with my rifle so I could get the jump on the police when they passed. First I realized these were free horses; then I realized they were Parenteau's, so I caught another mare and let the stallion go.

I put my wife on one of the mares but she had never ridden bareback, so I had to lead her horse with a rope. On the other mare I put a half-bag of flour that I had been carrying when I was leading the two horses. The stallion followed the two mares and wouldn't leave them. Finally I had to hit him hard with a stick to stop him.

We camped at the northeast edge of Belle Prairie. We spent the morning in the woods where we ate breakfast. I left my wife hidden there and went on foot to find Riel.

I climbed the bluffs, going from side to side, hiding in the smaller bluffs as I went. I saw a man hiding near the top of the bluff. It was a

Sioux, so I snuck up on him and spoke to him in Sioux. He was very surprised.

I kept looking for Riel. But I couldn't find where he was hiding, so I started calling him very loudly. Jim Short answered me from off to the side but he wouldn't come up to the prairie, so I went to him. Jim Short told me he had been trying to hide with his horse, but he was going to abandon it because he couldn't hide with it.

"I'll take it myself," I said.

"Take it," he said, and he untied the rope he had around his body and gave it to me. I went to get the horse and started calling for Riel again. This time, the three young Trottiers answered. They were looking for their mother. There were many Métis horses on the trail so I told them to take them, or the police would.

I returned to my wife with Jim Short's horse. The rest of the Métis were passing through there as they fled, so we followed them. When we arrived at Calixte Lafontaine's, we found Emmanuel Champagne's wife in a wagon. She told us that many people who had fled had passed by there. We went on and found the wife of Baptiste Parenteau, Riel's sister. We followed their tracks and caught up with them near Montour Butte, about ten miles away. There were ten women with Elie Dumont, Pierre Laverdure, and the son of Pierre Sansregret.

We camped with them, and the next day I left one of the mares with the women and gave the other to Alexandre Fageron, my adopted son. I was going to my father's, when I saw three policemen on the trail being escorted by some Indians. I had my rifle, as always. They were about three hundred yards away when the Indians saw me and told the police. The police knew my reputation for taking advantage of small enemy patrols, so they sent one of the Indians to talk to me. When he was close enough to speak, I ordered him to stop.

"Are you afraid of me?" asked the Indian.

"Certainly," I said. "How is it that yesterday you fought against the police, and today you help them look for me?"

"You have no reason to fear me."

"Don't come any closer or I will have to shoot you."

The policemen stayed at a distance. They wouldn't come any closer because they knew I wouldn't let them take me alive. I said to the

Indian, "I will not lay down my arms—I will fight forever. And the first who comes for me, I will kill." The Indian went back to the police and they left, no doubt to return with reinforcements. But they could not find me.

I went on to my father's and met J.B. Parenteau, who I gave my best horse, so he could save himself.

Moise Ouellette was at my father's. He had a letter for Riel and the others. He gave me the warrant, and I asked if he knew what was in it: "Give it to me and tell me what it says."

"Yes: they promise you justice, if you give yourself up with Riel," answered Moise.

"I will not surrender, but I will keep searching for Riel—not to make him surrender, but escape. If I find him before the law does, I won't let him surrender. I will find him first, Moise."

I did not see Riel again.

Sample page from the transcription of Dumont's dictations.
Library and Archives Canada, Ottawa.

APPENDIX

The Battle of Batoche, the Second or Third Day

The machine gun was set up on the prairie in front of the church, between the old and new trails.

I wanted to go and kill the gunner, so I told my men to let me approach; I would shoot him in the head and get rid of the machine gun. But my men at the front took two or three shots at the gun and didn't hit it. So they turned the machine gun in the direction of the fire. The branches were breaking all around me. I ended up crawling under the lowest branches, completely pinned down.

When I was in New York working for Buffalo Bill, a man who knew I was there came and asked for me, and told me, "I fought against you. I was a gunner. I fired the machine gun in front of the church. But that's all over: I am no longer against you. Even then I never shot at you, I only fired in the air, only to scare you. That's what I was hired for."

"I tried hard to kill you, when you were firing above our heads," I said, and told him the story of how I tried to put a bullet in his head, but all the branches were breaking around my head in that volley. He was an American from Montana. I was there during the war in the Transvaal and heard that he was killed there.

After Batoche

Father André said to the police, "You are looking for Gabriel? Well, you are wasting your time, there isn't a blade of grass on the prairie he does not know."

I did not want to surrender. I asked those who were surrendering to give me their bullets. I got eighty for my rifle and forty for my gun. I took the revolver from the sheriff, gave it to Monkman and then took it back again.

I wanted Riel to cross the line with me. I looked for him every day for four days. One time I called him from a bluff thinking he might be nearby. And that's right where he was—with the women and Nicolas Fageron, who recognized my voice. Riel thought it might be an English trap and would not answer.

Moise Ouellette took a letter from Middleton for Riel and me, asking us to surrender, promising us justice. Ouellette found me but I told him I would not surrender. Then he asked me where Riel was, and I said, "I am looking for him too, but I want to help him escape."

The fourth evening I ran into Ouellette again. He had lost his horse and asked me for one. "Well, that's strange," I answered. "You want me to give my horse to someone who now works for the government? Not on your life!" But all the same, I did direct him to the families camped near Bellevue who might give him a horse.

The fourth day Riel gave himself up. When I heard about it I decided to leave by myself.

I camped that night with Jean Dumont. I said my goodbyes and left. As I rode away someone yelled. It was Michel Dumas; he wanted to go with me. I thought about it, then told him he could come. Then he drank away the money given us by our American friends and lost their support.

During the four days I spent around Batoche, I did not go past Bellevue, about eight or ten miles away. Meanwhile, the plains were covered by enemy patrols looking for me. Each night I would camp at Batoche, and the next day I would wait for the patrols to leave and follow behind them. The whole day I was right behind them. From time to time I would stop at a bluff and wait while they scouted around, then I would go on. I knew the country like the back of my hand; I knew where to stop and where I would not be seen, so I just stayed right behind them while they searched. I had decided never to be taken alive. "I will never fall into their hands," I thought. I counted on my skill with horse and rifle and my cold-blooded will.

People thought that Riel surrendered in the end to save the lives of those who had fought with him, that he offered himself in their place. He thought they would be happy with his head.

Once during this time he said to his wife, "Oh, my poor Marguerite, I know the Good Lord wants me to die."

Before that, Riel had also said, "If it turns bad and the leaders are saved, there will be many followers who are lost." In prison he said, "I know that I will be pardoned by God, but not by men. Gabriel will be pardoned by both God and men."

Another time in prison, Riel was enlarging a hole he had found in the wooden door. As Joseph Delorme passed on his way to the toilet, Riel said to him, "When you come back, go slowly and do not look at me. I have something to ask you." Riel then asked him, "Do you know where Dumont is?"

He told Riel that I had crossed the line.

"Good," said Riel, "that will be good for all of you. You will go on living, but not me. You can depend on Dumont. He will travel all over, and be well-received everywhere he goes, and give great service to our people. I am going to die but he will live to a ripe old age."

Joseph Delorme, now at Dauphin, lost both testicles at the Battle of Batoche. The bullet also went through his thigh. He was found and looked after by the English. There were huge flaps of skin on both sides of the wound. To close it, they put him on a table and wanted to put him to sleep. He refused, and laughed while they operated to show he had no fear.

Michel Dumas and I Surrender to the American Police

When we got to Fort Assiniboine, we went at once to the authorities. We were put in the hands of a sergeant who made us follow him. He took us down a long hall and opened a door which led to a cell. He made us go in, and he locked the door behind us. "Well," I laughed, "this will be just fine. At least we don't have to sleep outside."

The sergeant returned soon, then quickly opened the door and made us come out. He excused himself because he had made a mistake—he was not supposed to put us in this cell, but the big room. The sergeant led us there, where an officer was waiting for us and was making new excuses.

Next we were taken to the fort's superior officer who spoke French. He told us he was going to telegraph the government about our case right away. We were well-treated there. The message to set us free came at two in the morning on the third day.

After Batoche

At the end we had taken about seventy rifles from the English.

A Frenchman, Paul Chelet, went to their camp and talked to an English officer, asking if he knew how many had been killed by their machine gun.

"No?"

"Well, I do," Chelet said.

"How many then? I would like to know."

"Well, just one."

"No—that's not possible."

"Yes, and it was my dog."

The officer was so mad he wanted to hit Chelet. He knew he would be mocked by the others.

Riel

When Riel heard blasphemy, he would always say, "Quick! Quickly—ask for God's pardon." One day he said this to a Métis who answered him, "Well, he never listens to me."

"That does not matter," said Riel. "You must not offend the Good Lord. You must ask. He will hear you and answer your prayers. So beg His pardon and mine as well."

"Pardon."

"You must take mass from only me."

Some of the priests were becoming impatient because Riel was discouraging the people from taking mass. Riel told them not to love the priests because they did not follow the law of God. "They only want to convert the world to make money," he told them.

The Arrest of Monkman after the Battle of Duck Lake

Riel said one day, "I have dreamed that there is a traitor among us and he wants to desert." Then he said to me, "In my dream the traitor was a short one." So it had to be Monkman. I also remembered the day we went to scout out on the other side of the crossroads near Duck Lake, and he was not where he was supposed to be. So he could have been the traitor. Riel asked me to call all the people together.

So I did as Riel asked and called everyone together. "I know that two of you have been asked to betray us. I want to know who they are and who asked them to desert."

But no one had been asked. As far as Riel was concerned, Monkman was guilty. So we arrested him and put him in the basement of Boyer's house beside his store.

The other prisoners were free in the room, but Monkman was chained by the leg up through the floor and around a small joist.

When we went to arrest Monkman, he tried to defend himself. He went for his revolver. I threw myself in front of the men who were trying to arrest him and grabbed his gun, telling him I would kill him if he moved. Scared, Monkman surrendered. I disarmed him, taking back the revolver I had given him before.

Between Duck Lake and Fish Creek

Riel spoke to a meeting at the church one day. "We must kill the English prisoners." There had been a man standing and he fell over in shock.

Another time Antoine Vandal had nearly lost his head and he begged me, "Cousin, I do not want to die." He was crawling after me, begging me.

Between Fish Creek and Batoche

My wife and Madame Batoche cared for the wounded.

One day Riel sent Jackson and the police prisoners to Duck Lake for safekeeping. When the Indians there saw the prisoners go by, they wanted their police scarves; it was all I could do to hold them back.

Cardinal died. He went mad first. Old Batoche found a piece of bone from his fractured skull in his pillow. We thought that the English prisoners had let some of the wounded die. I told Riel right then that the lives of the English prisoners were worth nothing, and they could no longer be trusted to care for the wounded.

A Sioux took care of the rifles at Batoche. He was very good at it.

Jim Swain made bullets with the lead from tea cases.

Generalities

The captains were William Boyer, Isidore Dumont, Augustin Laframboise, Calixte Lafontaine and Isidore Dumas. We left most of the goods in the stores and guarded them.

Duck Lake

Nolin the traitor fled in the buggy of the wife of his good brother-in-law, Attanase Lepine.

Many years later I met Nolin again and he said, "I am still your best friend. If I had to save myself it was because I was too scared." He also did not hold it against me that I wanted to shoot him when he fled to St. Laurent. He mentioned that I had been fair to everybody.

In 1903 Nolin told me I could stay with him until I died.

During Batoche, Nolin's wife and family stayed with Father Moulin.